Horses, Asses and Zebras in the Wild

Colin P. Groves

Horses, Asses and Zebras in the Wild

RALPH CURTIS BOOKS
HOLLYWOOD, FLORIDA
USA

To the memory of Erna Mohr

I.S.B.N. 0 88359-008-5

Library of Congress Catalog Number: 74-79610

Set in 11pt Garamond, 2pt leaded,
and printed in Great Britain
by Latimer Trend & Company Ltd Plymouth
for David & Charles (Holdings) Limited

First U.S. Edition
Published by:

RALPH CURTIS BOOKS
2633 Adams Street
Hollywood, Florida 33020
USA

Contents

	page
Acknowledgements	10
Introduction	13
1 The Horse Family	19
2 Wild Horses	50
3 Wild Asses	86
4 Zebras	123
5 Domestication	158
Appendices	
1 Classification of the Genus *Equus*	183
2 Species of Equids: Some Statistics	185
3 *Equus ferus* (Northern Pony)	186
4 Geographical Variations in Wild Asses and Zebras	187
Index	190

Illustrations

PLATES

page

Przewalski horse, *Equus ferus przewalskii* (Dr V. Mazák) 17

Reconstructed forest tarpan, *Equus ferus silvestris* (Dr V. Mazák) 17

The 'Munich breed' of steppe tarpan (author) 18

Exmoor ponies (the late Mrs M. G. Speed; courtesy Professor J. G. Speed) 18

Western kiang, *Equus kiang kiang* (the late Dr Erna Mohr) 35

Eastern kiang, *Equus kiang holdereri* (Dr V. Mazák) 35

Turkmenian wild ass or kulan, *Equus hemionus kulan* (Dr L. J. Dobroruka) 36

Indian wild ass, *Equus hemionus khur* (Dr Reuben David) 36

Syrian wild ass, *Equus hemionus hemippus* (the late Dr O. Antonius) 53

Nubian wild ass, *Equus africanus africanus* (author) 53

Somali wild ass, *Equus africanus somaliensis* (Zoological Society of London) 54

Cape mountain zebra, *Equus zebra zebra* (the late Dr Erna Mohr) 71

Hartmann's mountain zebra, *Equus zebra hartmannae* (Dr H. Klingel) 71

	page
The quagga, *Equus quagga* (Zoological Society of London)	72
Damara zebras, *Equus burchelli antiquorum* (Dr H. Klingel)	72
Grant's zebra, *Equus burchelli boehmi* (author)	89
Grévy's zebra, *Equus grevyi* (Dr H. Klingel)	89
The maneless zebra of Karamoja, north-eastern Uganda (author)	90
Somali wild asses (Dr H. Klingel)	107
Persian onagers, *Equus hemionus onager* (the late Dr Erna Mohr)	107
A kulan foal (Dr A. O. Solomatin)	108
A half-grown kulan in winter coat (Dr A. O. Solomatin)	108
Kulan on Barsa Kelmes (Dr V. A. Rashek)	125
Kulan during the rut (Dr A. O. Solomatin)	126
The Dziggetai of northern Mongolia, *Equus hemionus hemionus* (origin unknown)	126
Head of the Przewalski mare Orlitsa	143
Maneless zebra (Major F. Ziccardi)	144
Nubian wild asses (author)	144

LINE ILLUSTRATIONS

Fig		page
1	Skull and teeth of a Przewalski horse	21
2	Anatomical and colour pattern nomenclature of the Przewalski horse	26
3	Distribution of tarpans in Europe during historical times	68
4	Distribution in postglacial times of races of *Equus ferus*	75

Fig		page
5	Distribution of *Equus kiang*	95
6	Distribution of *Equus hemionus*	98
7	Recent distribution of *Equus africanus*	112
8	Distribution c 1800, of the four species of zebra	128
9	Distribution of Burchell's zebra	131
10	Known range of *Equus zebra*	146
11	Distribution of *Equus ferus*, in the late Würm glaciation	173
12	Variations in size through time of three species of wild horse	176

Acknowledgements

I would like to thank a number of people who have given me help in one way or another in the preparation of this book: by supplying photographs, sending information, sharing their knowledge, showing me their captive animals, or sometimes quite simply by discussions which have helped to clarify complicated issues. In alphabetical order, these are: W. F. H. Ansell, Lusaka; A. Azzaroli, Florence; Jeffrey Boswall, Bristol, England; Pat Carter, Cambridge, England; Reuben David, Ahmedabad, India; L. J. Dobroruka, Dvůr Kralove, Czechoslovakia; Peter Grubb, Accra; Th. Haltenorth, Munich; Dirk A. Hooijer, Leiden, Holland; Juliet Jewell, London, England; Hans Klingel, Braunschweig, Germany; J. M. Knowles, Marwell, England; Tony Legge, Cambridge, England; Charles A. Reed, Chicago; E. Schäfer, Hanover; J. G. Speed, Edinburgh; E. Trumler, Munich; Jiří Volf, Prague; Ferdinando Ziccardi, Bari, Italy.

Special mention must be made of my good friend and colleague, Vratislav Mazák (Prague, Czechoslovakia), with whom I have had so many fruitful discussions; and the late Erna Mohr, to whom this book is dedicated. Erna Mohr was one of those rare people to whom discovering the way things are, and saving rare animals, was a worthy aim, with no trace of egotism; she was delighted to be proved wrong because that is what progress in knowledge is all about; and she went out of her way to help aspiring youngsters and bring them together, to throw new light on old situations in the hope that it would help to save a unique product of nature for posterity.

Thou dost make springs break out in the gullies,
So that their water runs between the hills.
The wild beasts all drink from them,
The wild asses quench their thirst;
The birds of the air nest on their banks
And sing among the leaves.

Psalm 104, v 10–12

Introduction

There is something about a horse. Somehow, in the history of human cultures, horses have got under our skins; when we really needed them, depending on them for our transport and agriculture, they served us well and deserved our care and gratitude. Now that we need them less—some would say not at all—we appreciate them all the more.

It may be that what is happening is that we are keeping horses going against the day when we will need them again. We are gradually getting used to the idea that our dependence on machinery is only a transient phase in human history, and we will indeed require the horse in the future. Some breeds are already, it seems, making a minor comeback: at Britain's Midlands Shire Society's annual sale in 1971, the greatest sales of Shire horses were reported 'since the heyday of the horse'. Heavy machinery may damage the soil; as one farmer put it, it costs less to feed and house a pair of heavy horses than to do the same for a tractor; so, for all the admitted greater efficiency of farm machinery, the contest is not all one-sided. In Flanders, of course, the magnificent heavy horses they take such a pride in have never been entirely displaced, and have never ceased their labours before the plough.

And the horse shows; the pony clubs; the trekking holidays; the gymkhanas. These are a relatively new thing. Foxhunting on horseback has long been with us, and people have taken care in breeding their mounts for it; so have horseracing and polo. But never before has there been such a vast public for these pursuits.

Of course in the underdeveloped world, horses—not to mention asses and mules—have never lost their importance. Moreover some breeders are experimenting with new equid species, hybridising zebras with horses and asses, and their encouraging results suggest that these crosses too have a future.

Not surprisingly, the upsurge in the western world of interest in horses has brought with it an interest in their origins: where did our domestic horses and donkeys come from? What are their wild relatives like? How does a horse live when unsheltered and uncared for by man? Both laymen and scientists have been asking this question of late, and the answers that have begun to emerge are as fascinating as the more common-knowledge horse and pony lore. This book, then, is a study of wild horses and their relatives; those animals, now increasingly rare, that gave origin to our domestic breeds and for a while lived side by side with them. It is at the same time a plea for their conservation: not just a plea that they should not be maliciously shot or poisoned or disposed of as vermin, but an attempt to show that the causes of an animal's rarity goes deeper than human malice: it is a quite unintentional consequence of man's domination of the world.

The history of the tarpan shows this well enough. Once this tough grey pony was widespread in Europe; as the population of Europe increased, so more and more land was taken over for human habitation, grazing land for domestic animals, and agriculture. Where man moved in, wild horses moved out. The injunction 'Be fruitful and multiply', which our literal-minded ancestors happily obeyed, spelled doom to the tarpan; later on it spelled doom to the quagga and the Syrian wild ass, and nearly did so to the Przewalski horse (which survives only in captivity) and to the mountain zebra (which survives only in reserves).

It is all very well to point out that, if the tarpan had been preserved, the Poles and Ukrainians would have had a gene pool of hardy wild horses to draw upon to improve their tame stock; that the Boers would have kept a very useful reserve of meat on the hoof if they had been more thrifty with the quagga; that the Syrians would have had a good source of mule-breeding as the Kutch villagers do today. The point is that, more or less, these people had no option but to exterminate their wildlife: their populations were expanding, they needed the space for themselves and their domestic herds. When Moses gave his command to multiply, what he had in mind was certainly not the extermination of wild things: but that's the way it turned out. And inevitably so.

The horse family are a microcosm of the animal kingdom. Because they are large, mobile animals with heavy demands on the limited amount of food and space available, they are among the first to suffer when human demands for these same resources begin to increase. They were never scarce animals and the suggestion that equids, like other rare animals—rhinoceroses, whales, giant pandas, gorillas—were somehow on the way out anyway, dying on their feet, the last flickerings of a flame due to be soon snuffed out by some kind of evolutionary senescence, is sheer rubbish. With the possible exception of the giant panda, which does have a very restricted range but is none the less quite successful at exploiting it, all these animals were numerous and flourishing before they came into conflict with man. The plains of Cape Province teemed with quaggas; whales were stranded in hundreds on British shores alone; thousands of rhinoceros horns were exported each year from Borneo to China. How dare we call these animals on the way out? How can we possibly predict what would have happened to them if man had not interfered?

Once again I will emphasise that when I say 'interfered' I do not imply malice. It is an automatic process. As long as the human population continues to soar, and agriculture and urbanisation spread to cope with it, then we will see more extinctions of whole species. A few holding actions have been successful in staving off the evil day: most noticeably in the case of the Cape mountain zebra, which lives in a relatively well-watered part of South

Africa, where agriculture can be intensified before it has to be expanded, so that its habitat will not be overrun for many years. But the arid-country equids will not be so lucky; they are already gravely in conflict with stock-breeding interests, and except for a few less stressful areas they will soon disappear. First to go will be either the Indian wild ass, whose numbers are already perilously low, or Hartmann's mountain zebra, whose precipitous decline from 50,000 to 5,000 over the past twenty years leaves one speechless with shock. The Somali wild ass may survive for a while yet in Ethiopia, where protection is increasingly strict, but will vanish from Somalia. Onagers will cease to exist, perhaps before the end of the century, except in Badkhyz Reserve and in zoos. Grévy's zebra will soon be threatened; nobody knows anything of the present status of the kiang. Of all the wild equids, only Burchell's zebra has much of a foreseeable future; but, with East Africa's human population projected at four times its present level by the year 2000, how long will that last?

Yes, the horse family are the whole animal world in microcosm. Perhaps I have painted a deliberately gloomy picture: but this is the way things are going. And not through any evil intentions of ours: just because we do not think through the full consequences of our actions which seem harmless enough at the time. We kill the things we love—by thoughtlessness. What folly. We murder Nature, just as we are beginning to learn from her the things that could save us. What irony.

C.P.G.

Page 17   (above) *Przewalski horse,*
Equus ferus przewalskii: *the pure-
bred stallion 'Bars' in Prague zoo;*
(left) *the forest tarpan,* Equus ferus
silvestris, *as reconstituted by Polish
zoologists using koniks (Polish work-
ing ponies)*

Page 18　(above) The 'Munich breed', an attempt to reconstitute the steppe tarpan *Equus ferus ferus*, *in Brookfield zoo, Chicago. The domestic horses used in the experiment are probably not descended from the steppe tarpan*; (below) *Exmoor ponies, today maintained mostly in a semi-wild state, represent an almost pure-bred strain of aboriginal wild pony*

I The Horse Family

Horses and their relatives (the asses and zebras), the zoological family Equidae, are hoofed animals like those other familiar domesticates, cows and sheep; but scientific opinion for a long time now has held that the two groups are not closely related. Horses have only one hoof on each foot; and, as hooves are really hard keratinised toenails, we can see that they must have only one toe on each foot. Cows and sheep, on the other hand, are 'cloven-hoofed', implying that they have two toes on each foot not just one. This difference is a very basic one, and goes a very long way back in time; the horse and its relatives are known as the odd-toed hoofed animals, the zoological order Perissodactyla, while the cow and its relatives are the even-toed hoofed mammals, the order Artiodactyla.

The difference between the two orders does not relate so much to the different number of toes, but rather to the way weight-bearing is distributed between them. Primitive mammals, ancestors of both orders, had five toes on each foot and rested their weight equally around them; the ancestors of the Perissodactyla began to bear their weight on the central toe of each foot, while those of the Artiodactyla began to bear it on the central *two* toes. The side toes in each case thus became, more or less, superfluous weight, and so were lost; and the end-point of each line, the end-products of some 70 million years of evolution, today have come down to the irreducible minimum.

The Equidae are not the only living members of the odd-toed group: there are two other families. Surprisingly, at first sight, the rhinoceros belongs in this order—family Rhinocerotidae. Rhinos have not one, but three toes on each foot; their weight being borne primarily on the middle toe, the side ones playing an accessory role only. Their skeletons and muscles show, like those of horses, a fundamental adaptation to the central weight-bearing theme; the major difference is that they have retained the side toes, while horses have lost them. Horses are specialised as fast runners, so that any side toes on their slender limbs would be dead weight; whereas rhinos are heavy-bodied animals, and still need the side toes to help bear the weight of their tremendous bulk.

The third living family of the Perissodactyla is the family Tapiridae: the tapirs. These odd-looking, superficially pig-like animals from South-east Asia and Latin America are related to rhinos, but have retained even more of their side toes: their front feet each have four toes, although the hind feet have three like rhinos. The extra toe on the front foot is on the outside; the weight is borne, as in rhinos, on the big middle toe. If we give the toes numbers, the innermost—the one corresponding to the thumb or big toe in man—being I, the outermost V, then we see that all the Perissodactyla bear their weight primarily on toe III and have successively lost the rest; tapirs have lost I on their forefeet, I and V on their hindfeet; rhinos have lost I and V on all feet; and horses have lost I, II, IV and V on all their feet. However, rudiments of toes II and IV can still be seen as flattened splint bones on either side of the cannon and shannon bones of most equids. During the course of the family's evolution, as we shall see later, the side toes became smaller and smaller, until only these tiny rudiments remained.

TEETH

Their prime habitat is the open plains and their basic food grass, a tough siliceous herbage which wears down teeth rapidly. The horse's teeth, however, have become adapted to eating it in a way that counteracts its fast-wearing property: they are high-crowned, and the cheekteeth (molars and premolars—the grinding teeth) are complex in shape. Basically, teeth are made of dentine, a bone-like substance, with an outer coating of enamel. On the cheekteeth the enamel is folded into loops, giving a hard grinding surface; the valleys between the enamel ridges are filled with cementum, a substance not as hard and shiny as enamel, but more resistant than dentine. As the horse chews, the grass is minced up between the

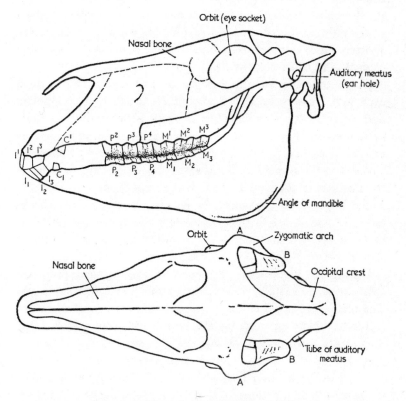

Fig 1 *Skull and teeth of a Przewalski horse*

enamel loops of the opposing sets of teeth into a small bolus which is then swallowed.

In front of the cheekteeth there is a gap, where there are no teeth: the diastema. This makes a convenient place to put the bit when fitting harness, although in the wild there are several reasons why this gap exists. One is, that it lengthens the jaws without increasing the number or size of the teeth, so enabling the horse to reach the ground and graze while the eyes are still high enough to keep watch for danger. The anterior teeth are called the incisors; they are long and roughly cylindrical, with no enamel loops on them, and they are used for cropping grass— or for biting rivals or enemies. Just behind them, in stallions, are shorter, more pointed teeth, the canines; mares have only tiny canines, and often none at all.

There are three incisors, one canine and seven cheekteeth in each half of each jaw. The cheekteeth are divided into premolars and molars; there is no difference in shape between the two kinds —the reason they are classed differently will become obvious below. The initial letters I, C, P and M are used when referring to these teeth, with a number written above or below to indicate the position in the jaw. Thus, I^1 is the upper central incisor; M_3 is the lower third (posterior) molar. In the case of the cheek-teeth, P^1 and P_1 are tiny, peg-like teeth which are generally lost early in life; the rest are large complicated teeth as described above.

During the lifetime of a horse, as of any mammal, there are two sets of teeth: milk, or deciduous teeth, and permanent teeth. The milk teeth begin to erupt before birth; they are shed before maturity, being replaced by the permanent teeth which erupt underneath them as they fall out, one by one. The molars are not preceded by milk teeth, whereas the premolars are: this is the essential difference between them. When referring to milk teeth in the shorthand notation, we simply add D (for deciduous) before the letters.

At birth, the foal's central milk incisors (I^1 and I_1) have already erupted. In a week or so its three milk premolars begin to appear. After 2 months, DI^2_2 are cut; DI^3_3 in 6–8 months; and DC (the milk canines) at the same time, but they do not usually cut through the gum. The first two incisors, in both jaws, are shaped much like flattened ice-cream cones, with a rim of enamel at the biting edge, surrounding an oval central space (the infundibulum or 'mark'); the third incisors are similar but their cutting edges slope down to the outer side instead of being horizontal. All the milk incisors have begun to wear down by the end of the first year, and shortly afterwards they have ground down sufficiently so that the outer edges of DI^3_3 have become level with the rest of the cutting edge.

Between a year and 18 months the first permanent molar (M^1_1) erupts; and around 2 years of age, M^2_2 appear. At about $2\frac{1}{2}$ years, DI^1_1 begin to loosen; they are quickly shed, and the first permanent incisors (I^1_1) erupt in their place. These, like the deciduous incisors, have a ring of enamel around a central infundibulum; as the tooth wears, the enamel on the biting surface wears away, revealing a softer, yellowish substance underneath—dentine. Therefore an incisor, after a year or so of wear, acquires a flat table on the biting surface with a hole in the middle: the table is made of dentine, with an enamel rim round the edge, and enamel rimming the infundibulum.

At 3 years, M^3_3 erupts, and the permanent premolars push through to replace the milk ones. The little peg-like P^1_1 may erupt at this time, but it often does not appear at all, or else it appears briefly and is then shed. This is the tooth often referred to as the 'wolf tooth'. The second permanent incisors I^2_2, erupt at $3\frac{1}{2}$ years, and have begun to wear off their enamel caps, forming a flat table like I^1_1, at 4 years. Meanwhile DI^3_3 have been worn down to a stump and are shed and replaced at $4\frac{1}{2}$ years. The canines, which are large in males and hardly developed at all in females, appear along with I^2_2.

Once all the permanent teeth have erupted, it is their patterns that must be used in estimating age. The infundibula are elongated oval cavities when the tooth erupts, but as the incisors wear down, the shape gets shorter and broader. Obviously as a tooth wears down, structures that began life low down, deep inside the tooth, appear on the upper surface because what was above them has been worn away. Since the infundibula in an unworn incisor are oval at the top, getting smaller and narrower farther down the tooth until they finally end, it is perfectly reasonable that the 'mark' on the wear table should appear to change shape: at the ages 3–5 the 'mark' is long and narrow on all incisors; by 6 years, that on I_1^1 has become short and broad; and by 7 years it has become short and broad on I_2^2 as well. The 'mark' finally disappears from I_1^1 at 10 years, and from I_2^2 at 12 years. As for I_3^3, the shape and size of the infundibulum are more variable, often the back of the tooth does not close so that it is slightly cupped, the infundibulum being open behind—forming a notch instead of a hole.

After the infundibula have worn out, a horse can still be aged by 'Galvayne's mark', a depression on the outer surface of I_3^3, which appears at the gum line at 10 years of age and gradually works its way down the tooth as the incisor is worn off from the top, and the gum recedes from the bottom. At 15 years it is half-way down the outer surface of the tooth; at 20 years it reaches the biting surface; at 25 years half of it has worn out; at 30 years it has disappeared.

As the gum-line recedes with age, the incisors slope more and the shape of their wear tables becomes more triangular, less oval. The canines, initially sharp, become rounded. The cheekteeth, like the incisors, are capped with enamel when they erupt. As they wear the surface enamel is worn off revealing a wear table of dentine, with a wavy enamel rim round it, and two areas are surrounded by enamel—the fossettes—within this rim. The shapes of the enamel folds, on both the outer rim and the fossette rims, are tolerably constant; within limits, it is generally possible to distinguish between horses, asses and different species of zebras by these shapes.

Asses and zebras can be aged the same way as horses, by their incisors. Zebras, however, seem to go through the sequence more quickly than horses, being in the early stages about half a year ahead of horses, and in their teens and twenties as much as 2–3 years ahead. In the quagga, like the horse, infundibula were present on all three incisors of both jaws; but in Grévy's zebra and the mountain zebra, those on I_3 (in the lower jaw) are not fully closed behind; in asses, I_2 may also be partly open behind. Burchell's zebra very often lacks the infundibula on all three lower incisors, so that their wear tables are simple elongated ovals: those from southern Africa may have complete, closed infundibula on I_1 and I_2, but more usually have a simple depression on the back surface; those from East Africa never have anything more than a depression—if at all.

THE SHAPE OF A HORSE

The skull of a horse is long and narrow, with a long face to contain the battery of cheekteeth. The orbits (eye-sockets) are prominent—more so in horses and asses than in zebras—and look out to the side, so that the horse can scan the horizon to watch for danger. However, he cannot see stereoscopically because the fields of vision of the two eyes do not overlap. His visual sweep is increased by the shape of the pupils, which are oblong and horizontal.

The nostrils are large and mobile, and can be closed tight against dust-storms. The lips too are mobile, and can be drawn back in different ways to give quite a variety of facial expression. The ears are moved back and forth, not only to catch sounds but also as a means of communication.

The neck, long and supple, can be raised as the nostrils test the wind, lowered to let the animal graze, or twisted into a variety of positions so that the horse can bite his itches. The mane runs along the back of the neck: soft, falling to one side in horses, but stiff and upright in asses and zebras. The Mongolian wild horse is an exception to this, having an upright mane, and it seems probable that some other wild types did as well.

A running animal, like the horse, has to breathe deeply, and needs a deep chest. The rib-cage is deep and narrow, with the forelegs articulated on it to the front and at the side. The shoulder-blades are therefore on the side of the chest, not on the back as

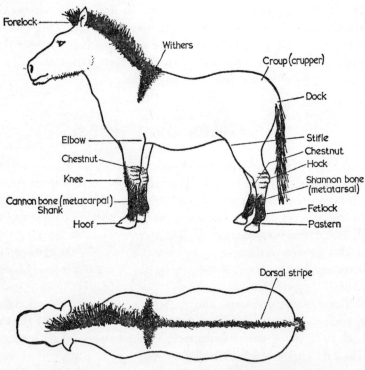

Fig 2   *Anatomical and colour pattern nomenclature of the Przewalski horse*

in man; and there are no clavicles (collar-bones). The back, between the withers (point of the shoulder) and croup (point of the rump), is concave—'sway-backed'. The shape of the croup itself varies according to the type of equid and the sort of environment it inhabits: thus the croup of asses, which in the wild live in stony desert country, is high and angular, while that of horses is broad and rounded.

The legs taper down to the hooves, so as to reduce the weight lifted during walking or running. Humerus (upper arm) and femur (thigh) are bound into the body wall; they can be seen moving under the skin as the animal walks. This certainly helps to keep the legs in position under the body for support and to prevent them splaying out to the side. The foreleg does not leave the body above the elbow; and the hindleg is bound to it as far as the stifle (which corresponds to the knee, in man).

The central joints of the legs of a horse are, therefore, not the elbow and knee like man, but the wrist and ankle. The wrist (carpus) of a horse, confusingly referred to as the knee because it bends forward, is composed of several bones like the wrist of other animals. Below it, the shank consists of a single bone, the metacarpus or cannon-bone; this corresponds to the central bone of the palm in man, and as explained earlier it generally has splint-bones on either side, tiny rudiments of two other metacarpals. In the hindleg, the ankle (tarsus), is referred to as the hock, and below it is the shannon-bone or metatarsus, again with splint-bones.

Just as man has three bones, placed end to end, in his middle finger and middle toe, so does the horse. The first two are small, cuboid bones; the third one, which bears the hoof, is broad and high, triangular from the side and semicircular from below. Externally, therefore, the limb suddenly narrows below the shank, then broadens again at the hoof. The narrow portion is called the pastern, the broad part above it (the lower end of the shank) is known as the fetlock.

The hoof, hard and blackish or rimmed with yellow, varies in shape like the croup. Most horses have a broad, rounded lower rim to the hoof, and so do some zebras; but asses and the mountain zebra have high, narrow hooves making them very sure-footed in their rocky habitat.

On the inner aspects of the knees and hocks of horses are hard, hairless wart-like excrescences, the chestnuts. They are long and fairly narrow, or oval. Asses, zebras and a few breeds of domestic horses have them on the forelegs only, and they tend to be smaller. Just under the fetlocks there are much smaller warts, the ergots; these occur in all equids except for some domestic horse breeds.

Asses and zebras have a longish, tufted tail like most other hoofed animals. The horse's tail looks quite different. In most domestic horses the whole tail is clothed in long flowing hair extending from the root. In some breeds, and in the Przewalski wild horse, the long hairs do not begin at the root itself but a few inches down; while one of the wild asses, the kiang, has longer hairs going up the side of the tail towards the root. There are thus intermediate forms between the typical horse and zebra types.

THE KINDS OF HORSES

This very general description of the equid has, I hope, brought out the features that are in common between all living horses, asses and zebras, and at the same time touched upon some differences between them. The living equids are all so fundamentally similar that they are placed in one genus, *Equus*. There are eight living species, differing in various features like their colour pattern, form of mane and tail, chestnuts, body size, hoof shape, and features of the skull and teeth, but they all share the same general body build, specialised for running and the same skull shape, specialised for grazing and so on. No other living mammal has even remotely similar combinations of characteristics; the rhinos and tapirs seem to have stopped off halfway, while the Artiodactyla have done the same thing in quite a different way. Fossil equids, as we shall see, show the intermediate stages towards the specialisations of *Equus*, and are put in different genera (the plural of genus).

The eight living species are not all equally related, and their species names are usually just added on to the generic name— *Equus hemionus* for the Asiatic wild ass, *Equus zebra* for the mountain zebra, and so on. When we want to show different degrees of relationship we can divide up the genus into subgenera, allotting species to each one. The names of the subgenera are made part of the species' names by inserting them, in parentheses, after the generic name. This will be made clear by looking at the classification of *Equus*:

The Genus *Equus*
> First subgenus: *Equus*, the horses
>> Species: *Equus (Equus) ferus*, Przewalski's (Mongolian) wild horse
> Second subgenus: *Asinus*, the asses
>> Species: *Equus (Asinus) kiang*, the kiang, or Tibetan wild ass
>> *Equus (Asinus) hemionus*, the onager, or Asiatic wild ass
>> *Equus (Asinus) africanus*, the African wild ass
> Third subgenus: *Hippotigris*, the common zebras
>> Species: *Equus (Hippotigris) zebra*, the mountain zebra
>> *Equus (Hippotigris) quagga*, the quagga (now extinct)
>> *Equus (Hippotigris) burchelli*, Burchell's zebra
> Fourth subgenus: *Dolichohippus*, Grévy's zebra
>> Species: *Equus (Dolichohippus) grevyi*, Grévy's zebra.

Not every student of the Equidae ('hippologists' if you like) agrees that this is the best classification. Some think that the kiang is just a race, or variety, of the ordinary Asiatic wild ass, so do not recognise it as a species; similarly, others consider that Burchell's zebra is just a race of the quagga. As we shall see below, what is a species and what is not has an objective basis and should be provable as a fact. The difficulties arise, however, when the facts are not quite clear.

More subjective is the question of genera and subgenera. Here, it is a matter of opinion what rank in classification we allot certain species groupings. Some authorities would give the kiang and the onager a subgenus of their own, *Hemionus*, separating them from the African wild ass; others would refuse to set Grévy's zebra apart in its own subgenus, but would sink it into *Hippotigris*. A different school of thought would make these groupings not subgenera, but genera; so we would refer to *Asinus africanus*, *Hippotigris burchelli*—even, sometimes, *Hemionus hemionus*! However, it can be argued that the differences are not really so great; that all the eight species are fundamentally alike; and that members of the genus *Equus* can be recognised in the fossil record only for about 5 million years—a standard length of time for any genus of mammals. To draw a parallel case, the different species of rhinoceros are far more distinctive than are those of living equids; their skeletons can be instantly distinguished from one another, which those of equids cannot without detailed examination; and some of them were already distinct as long ago as 12 million years. The living species of rhinos are rightly placed in four genera; those of equids are best placed in only one.

Some of the differences between the different equids have already been mentioned; others are more subtle, consisting of tooth patterns or skull proportions. The subgenus *Equus* (horses) is distinguished by its long-haired tail, chestnuts on all four limbs (usually), no body-stripes, its distinctive colour pattern (dark shanks, underside not lighter than upperside), large cheek-teeth, high muzzle, protruding orbits and various other features. The subgenus *Asinus* (asses) shows many features in common with horses, but the tail is short-haired, chestnuts are confined to the forelimbs, the underside and legs are light to white, the ears are long, the cheekteeth are smaller, and the muzzle lower. The subgenus *Hippotigris* (most of the zebras) is more like *Asinus*, but the body is striped, partly or wholly, the orbits do not protrude, and the teeth differ in pattern. Finally in *Dolichohippus* (Grévy's zebra) the stripe pattern is very unlike that of other zebras, the ears are very long and broad, the skull is extremely long and narrow, and they have a distinctive teeth pattern.

Bodily proportions also vary from one species to another. The shanks are very long and narrow in Burchell's zebra and in some of the onagers and the kiang; they are shorter (compared to the upper segments of the limbs) in the quagga and Grévy's zebra; and still shorter in horses, African wild asses, and the mountain zebra. The head is large, compared to the rest of the body, in horses and the kiang; less so in most other equids; and is small compared to the body in the mountain zebra. The intestine is 17 times the body length in mountain and Burchell's zebras, 15 times in horses, and only 11–12 times in asses and Grévy's zebra. The hoof is broad and rounded in horses and kiangs, fairly broad in Burchell's and Grévy's zebras, narrower in onagers and most of the African wild asses, and very narrow and high in mountain zebras and certain other races of asses. These are all examples of characters which do not vary between subgenera, but rather haphazardly between different species.

Another characteristic which has been studied recently, and has been found to differentiate between species, very neatly, is the number of chromosomes. These are the small thread-like bodies found in every cell of the body, which carry the hereditary particles or genes. They are big enough, at some stages of the cell's development, to be seen under the microscope, and then their number can be counted and their shape examined. It is found that Przewalski's horse has 66 chromosomes, domestic horses have 64, onagers have 54 or 56, African wild asses and domestic donkeys have 62, Grévy's zebra has 46, Burchell's zebra 44, and the mountain zebra only 32. Just what the significance of the differences may be, is unknown; presumably the same amount of genetic material is present in each species, but differently arranged. For example, the chromosomes of mountain zebras are larger than the more numerous chromosomes of horses. No one has yet looked at the chromosomes of the kiang; and, alas, it is too late for us ever to see those of the quagga.

SPECIES AND THEIR HYBRIDS

When we say that two forms are distinct species, it means that, under natural conditions, they do not interbreed. In South-West Africa (Namibia) both mountain and Burchell's zebras occur in the same habitat, but when they meet they do not interbreed. Similarly, in northern Kenya and southern Somalia, Grévy's and Burchell's zebras occur together and even form mixed herds, but no hybrids are produced. All zebras therefore, can at once be distinguished as particular species: there are no hybrids. In former days, it seems that quaggas lived side by side in Cape Province with both mountain and Burchell's zebras; Grévy's zebra with wild asses in northern Somalia; onagers with Przewalski horses in Mongolia. No hybrids seem ever to have been reported in the wild.

But when animals are taken out of their natural habitat, and forced into unnatural proximity with each other in captivity or domestication, then species which would not dream of inter-breeding in the wild, will do so. Probably mate availability has something to do with it; if a horse and a donkey are put together for breeding purposes, they must be alone, and no alternative members of the same species should be present. However, hybrids obtained by crossing different species of equids are almost always sterile. And, even though onagers and mountain zebras never meet in the wild so that we cannot test whether they will hybridise under natural conditions, the fact that hybrids between them produced in captivity are sterile implies that they are in any case 'reproductively isolated'.

Traditionally it is said, when crossing horses and asses, that the characters of the sire come out in the extremities (ears, tail, feet). Thus, a mule, the offspring of a jack-ass and a mare, has a short thick head, long ears, a short mane, thin legs, narrow hooves, a tufted tail and no hindlimb chestnuts, like an ass; in size, shape of neck and croup, and the uniform colour of its coat, it is like a horse. Since mules are large but narrow-hoofed, they are not only strong but sure-footed, and can pack very heavy loads especially over mountainous country. The reverse cross, between a stallion and a she-ass, is called a hinny or jennet; it is smaller and more horselike than a mule, with shorter ears, a larger head and broader hooves; but has the ass's disruptive colour pattern and stripes. In spite of its small size it is quite strong, and said to make an excellent riding animal. Mules and hinnies have 63 chromosomes—halfway between horses and asses.

It was Raymond Hook, a well-known horse-breeder, of Nanyuki on the slopes of Mount Kenya, who first thought of breeding zebroids (zebra-horse hybrids) for commercial purposes, using a Grévy's zebra stallion and horse mares. They resemble horses more in their conformation, but have tufted tails, and they usually take on the mother's colour characteristics. However, zebroids do have the fine narrow stripes of the father, more prominent on the face and legs. A few crosses have also been made the other way round; the difference between the two types is not as great as that between mules and hinnies, but merely a matter of how well expressed the stripes are. These are emphasised more when the sire is a zebra. Like mules, the hybrids are strong and docile, and they have been trained to carry packs up Mount Kenya for climbers; unlike mules, they are not markedly intelligent.

Other types of hybrids have been obtained—usually, fairly easily. Those with zebras as one parent tend to have the stripes well expressed on the face and limbs, less so on the body, and the stripes are rather finer and more numerous than in the zebra parent; the general body colour resembles the non-zebra parent. All are sterile, with the exception of very occasional mules; all, however, are perfectly strong and vital. The only exception to this is that hybrids involving Grévy's zebra are often aborted during development. Temperament and conformation are intermediate between the parents. Some have been very long-lived; for example, a male hybrid between a Przewalski stallion and a Burchell's zebra mare, born in Askania Nova Park, USSR, in 1929, was reported still living in 1963.

And what of those that are fertile? A few female hybrids between asses and Burchell's zebras have been reported as being fertile, but nothing has been recorded about the backcross. But for mules, there is information that a very few, probably under 1 per cent and females only, have been fertile. The offspring of a mule and a stallion is a mule or a horse; the offspring of a mule with a jack-ass is a mule or an ass!

Why? Here we must go back to chromosomes. When sex cells (sperms in males, ova in females) are formed, the chromosomes which are paired in all other body cells are halved. That is to say, a horse—which has 64 chromosomes, composed of 32 pairs—would form sperms and ova containing 32 chromosomes only. When mating occurs, a 32 chromosome sperm from the stallion unites with a 32 chromosome ovum in the mare, bringing the number up again to 64. Because the chromosomes from each set are the same size and shape, when the offspring itself comes to form sperm or ova the two sets of chromosomes mix and exchange material. When a jack-ass (62 chromosomes) mates with a mare (64 chromosomes), the 31 chromosome sperm unites with the 32 chromosome ovum to form a mule, with 63 chromosomes; but the ass and horse chromosomes are different not only

Page 35 (above) *Western kiang*, Equus kiang kiang, *in Munich zoo, 1933;* (below) *Eastern kiang*, Equus kiang holdereri—*a young male who died recently in Prague zoo. Eastern kiangs are larger than Western kiangs, lighter in colour with a greater extent of white areas on the body*

Page 36 (above) *Turkmenian wild ass or kulan*, Equus hemionus kulan, *in Prague zoo. Note the broad dorsal stripe, bordered on both sides with a white seam;* (below) *Indian wild asses*, Equus hemionus khur, *in their natural habitat. This race is nearing extinction in the wild*

in number but in size and shape too, so that they are incompatible and no genetic material can be exchanged between them. There is, therefore, difficulty, for this and other reasons, in forming sex cells in mules. But occasionally a female mule does form ova, by means of separating the whole horse set from the whole ass set —essentially, therefore, she produces horse ova and ass ova. In this case, if mated to a horse, she can give birth to a horse or a mule, if mated to an ass she can produce a mule or an ass. All backcrosses that have been recorded are either mules themselves, or—and this does seem more common—indistinguishable from the sire. The three-quarter hybrid is not three-quarters in appearance.

When Cyrus the Great, emperor of the Medes and Persians, was besieging Babylon which had revolted from his rule, the impregnable city had stocked up with abundant provisions and was all set to withstand siege for a good long time. The walls were high and thick, and a Babylonian shouted down scornfully at the Persian army, 'Cyrus will never take Babylon—not till mules have foals!' This, of course, was tempting fate. In the Persian encampment, a mule gave birth to a foal, and not long afterwards Babylon was taken by means of a trick.

To return to the matter of hybrids, and their bearing upon species difference. If two species hybridise and the hybrids are not themselves fertile, it is clear that as far as their natural relationships are concerned they are 'reproductively isolated'. The opposite case does not hold, however: if two species interbreed and form fertile hybrids in captivity, it does not therefore follow that they are not reproductively isolated in the wild. The reasons they do not form hybrids in the wild may have nothing to do with any genetic incompatibility, which is what is implied by hybrid sterility. The two species may have different courtship behaviours; they may have colour or shape characters which, right from the start, inhibit cross-breeding. This is worth remembering, and will become important when we consider the

C

origin of the domestic horse, which could well be derived from different wild ancestral species.

THE PROBLEM OF DOMESTICATION

Domestic horses and asses are not included among the eight species of living equids, nor were they even mentioned earlier when talking about classification. The reason for this is simple: they do not exist as entities in the same way as the wild species do. They may well have been derived by cross-breeding different wild races, even perhaps different species; they do not live under natural conditions, where the environment will select the fittest individuals to survive and impose a certain uniformity on them; and breeds are maintained or crossed purely at the whim of man, who alone enforces reproductive isolation. For these reasons they are not considered nowadays in zoological classifications.

Of course, scientific names have in the past been applied to domestic animals. The domestic horse has been called *Equus caballus*. This is a construct, an artificial category which includes Arabians, Percherons and Shetlands and it is possible to distinguish them all from donkeys, but not from Przewalski horses. Similarly, you can distinguish all domestic donkeys—'*Equus asinus*'—from horses, dut not from African wild asses. Policy is therefore simply to ignore them when classifying the wild forms, but to bring them into consideration when studying how many of these wild forms there must have been, and how they have been modified and cross-bred to bring them into domestication.

THE EVOLUTION OF THE HORSE

When we go back into the past to see how horses have come to be what they are today, we see a story of gradual unfolding of the running and grazing specialisations. The earliest of the Perissodactyla came from the early Eocene Age, 55 million years ago: the little *Hyracotherium*.

Under a foot high, with short face and rounded haunches, *Hyracotherium* was quite unlike any living odd-toed hoofed mammal; yet it was certainly very close to the common ancestor of horses, tapirs and rhinos. Its remains were first found in European rocks, and later turned up in North America as well; the American finds were at first given a separate generic name, *Eohippus* ('dawn horse'), but when they were compared with the European form they were found to be the same. This may seem surprising at first, but when we remember that the continents have drifted about the surface of the globe, it becomes explicable. It is now clear from geological evidence that at this time, Europe was separated from Asia by a seaway, about where the Urals now are, but joined to North America via Greenland, Iceland and Rockall, which was then dry land above water. Rather more surprising, this whole land mass enjoyed a tropical climate. The little horse-ancestor scuttled around on the forest floor, browsing for low shrubs. It had already lost the two side toes on its hindfeet, and the inner one of its forefeet, and so resembled the tapir; the metacarpals and metatarsals were still independent of each other, like those of the palm of the hand and sole of the foot in man. Probably the feet were held at any angle to the ground—not vertically as in modern equids—and had pads to rest the toes on, like a dog.

The teeth of *Hyracotherium* were low-crowned, not at all like those of modern horses, and without the complex enamel ridges on the cheekteeth: in fact, without ridges at all, but simple high conical cusps. The cheekteeth were small, the muzzle short, the incisors low and simple, and the canines relatively larger than in modern horses. The tail was very long, and held in a curve like a cat's. Indeed the general appearance would have been much more like a small cat or dog than any hoofed animal.

Shortly after this time, several lines of descent separated from the equid line. If not descended from *Hyracotherium*, they certainly came from something very like it. One of these led to the rhinos and tapirs; very early on, they acquired the basic characters they possess today, and although some rhinos—especially the white rhinoceros of Africa—are highly specialised in their own right, others like the Sumatran rhinoceros and most of the tapirs emerged early on and have remained much the same ever since. Two other lines separated about this time; one of them, the Brontotheroidea, quickly became gigantic in size (the largest of them almost the size of an elephant), with a symmetrically forked bony 'horn' on the nose. They flourished and died down, becoming extinct about 30 million years ago. The other line also became quite large but remained slenderly built: the Chalicotheroidea. Instead of cutting down their side toes and keeping their hooves, they developed enormous claws on their feet. Undoubtedly these were for digging; they would probably have fed on roots and bulbs which they scraped out of the earth with their claws. The chalicotheres underwent a less spectacular evolution than the brontotheres, and lasted almost up to the present day—that is, to about 1 million years ago. Then they too died out: just why, we cannot say.

In the middle and upper Eocene, up to about 36 million years ago, horses essentially unchanged from *Hyracotherium* held sway. These genera, *Orohippus* and *Epihippus*, were larger with rather more complex teeth, but no different in their limbs or the mode of locomotion. These primitive creatures are all classified in a special subfamily of the Equidae, called Hyracotheriinae.

In the next epoch, the Oligocene, beginning about 38 million years ago, a new group of equids, the subfamily Anchitheriinae, evolved. Although descended from hyracotheriines, they differed in a number of ways. They had lost the fourth toe on the front feet, the lateral metacarpals and metatarsals were less independent, often free only at their lower ends, and the flexibility of movement at the fetlock was somewhat restricted, so that side-to-side move-ment was sacrificed in favour of fore-and-aft movement. All these changes represent advances towards the running way of life, but they were still extremely primitive in other ways: they probably had pads on the feet, the central toe was still relatively short, some lateral movement at the fetlock was still possible; the lateral toes still touched the ground and probably functioned in weight-bearing; and the foot slanted to the ground at an angle of 50°.

In the Miocene, beginning 24 million years ago, the environ-ment began to change. There may have been some desiccation, and certainly the climate was becoming more seasonal, squeezing the tropical zone towards the equator; but the main change was the sudden abundance of a group of plants—the Gramineae, or grasses. This formerly inconspicuous group underwent rapid evo-lutionary changes and spread all over the earth, replacing forests in many places. A new environment was now opened up on the grassy plains. Instead of open spaces being barren or sporadically dotted with vegetation, there were now wide areas with con-tinuous grass cover, and a great many groups of animals found it worthwhile adapting to a life in such areas. Grass is a much tougher, more fibrous material than leaves, and contains silica which scores and wears down teeth rather rapidly. The new grazing animals therefore needed tall, high-crowned cheek-teeth to cope with it, and long strong incisors to crop it—those that failed to develop these specialisations would simply have been unable to survive in such an environment. Additionally, the wide open spaces put a premium on adaptations to avoid danger, hence, large laterally directed eyes to survey the horizon, and slender well-knit feet to run fast away from it. And, since a large body-size is more economical in terms of nutrition and body heat than a small one, the grazing animals would be able to increase in size now that they no longer needed to stay small to slip under branches in the forest.

It is not surprising, therefore, that the equids which invaded the grassland habitat evolved very rapidly to fill their new niche. The subfamily Hipparioninae, as they are called, were still three-toed, but the central toe was lengthened, lifting the foot from the ground; there were no longer any pads; the fetlock was supported by a complex system of ligaments making it more flexible in a fore-and-aft direction, less so from side to side; and the lateral toes were firmly bound to the central one. Probably the side toes would still have functioned on soft ground, helping to spread the weight of the body; on hard ground, they may perhaps still have played a part in guiding the movements of the central toe. Their teeth were larger and more complex, and for the first time the cusps were united into long ridges, with cement between. The face was elongated to contain the battery of cheekteeth; there was a big gap between the cheekteeth and the incisors. These were, in other words, the first equids that really looked like horses.

The Hipparioninae were a highly successful group, and rapidly replaced the last remaining Anchitheriines; of this latter group just one or two hung on (presumably as forest-dwelling forms) into the Miocene. The anchitheriines had spread from North America, where they had evolved, into Eurasia, and now the Hipparionines did the same. Horses of the genus *Hipparion* seem to have arrived in Eurasia about 15 million years ago; they were abundant and widespread, and evidently a very successful type, since they survived virtually unchanged almost until the present day. A closely related form, *Stylohipparion*, lived until about 1 million years ago in South Africa, alongside the direct ancestors of modern zebras.

But in the late Miocene, perhaps about 10 million years ago, the ancestors of the modern horses, asses and zebras—the sub-family Equinae—evolved. Very similar to hipparionines, and obviously derived from them, they had completely lost their lateral toes; the foot was now held perpendicular to the ground; the bones of the last remaining toe were elongated, lifting the leg still higher; and the strong 'springing ligaments' of the fetlock were fully developed. A few changes in the cheekteeth, involving an increase in the enamel loops, completed the transition. The equines, too, spread throughout the New World, where they had evolved, and all through the Old World, though as we have seen they did not finally replace *Hipparion* and its relatives for a long time.

The impression is often given that the whole of horse evolution, from *Hyracotherium* to *Equus*, was a slow steady gradual change, going constantly in one direction. It was not like this at all, but proceeded in fits and starts. While the environment remained the same, so did the equids; when it changed, they changed too, taking advantage of the new conditions. It is important to realise that animals do not just carry on evolving due to some inner urge; they change in response to a change in the environment, and after a period of 'consolidation' when they improve and refine their initial adaptations to the new conditions, there is an essential marking time. Nor is evolution always in a straight line: within reason, changes can be reversed. The four sub-families of the Equidae represent successive points of environmental alteration when rapid evolution placed the equids on a new adaptive plateau.

THE FOSSIL ZEBRAS

What of the origin of modern species? There has been some argument over this recently. Traditionally, due to the work of G. G. Simpson and others, the view has held sway that the different species arose fairly recently, from an ancestor that was already single-toed (monodactyl), with high-crowned (hypsodont) cheekteeth and so on. More recently, J. H. Quinn claimed to have found evidence that horses, asses and zebras were separate lines already in the middle Miocene, about 12–15 million years ago, descended from ancestors with three toes and low-crowned cheekteeth, so that they must have independently acquired mono-dactyly, hypsodonty, and a number of special features of the cheekteeth. He made this claim on the evidence of many teeth, and a few skulls and limb-bones, from fossil beds in Texas, thought to be middle Miocene in age. However, this theory has been doubted by some: there is, for one thing, much more variability in dental patterns than used to be thought, and it is very difficult indeed to identify an isolated tooth as horse, ass or zebra. Secondly, some of the fossil beds that Quinn thought were so old turn out to be much younger than he supposed: those containing zebras, for example, are only about 5 million years old, or less, and at this time equids are known already to have become single-toed.

One of Quinn's discoveries does remain rather remarkable: a creature called *Eoequus wilsoni*, known from a complete skull and other remains from about 10 million years ago. The skull was like that of a small zebra, the teeth varied between horse-like and zebra-like forms, there was a lot of cement on the cheek-teeth, and hypsodonty was well advanced. In more primitive equids, one of the infoldings of the enamel rim round the cheek-teeth—the protocone—is disconnected, forming an enamel ring all by itself; in *Eoequus* the protocone was separate in unworn teeth, but joined the main rim lower down—an intermediate stage. It was from such a beast that *Equus* evolved.

Following upon this, equids seemed to undergo a diversifica-tion. In North America, about 5 million years ago, we have a giant form, *Dinohippus*, still three-toed; there were still many Hipparionines, large and small; and the first zebras emerged. Formerly referred to a subgenus *Plesippus*, it is now recognised that these zebras were quite closely related to the living Grévy's zebra, and have to be placed in the subgenus *Dolichohippus*. Not long after, in the late Pliocene ($3\frac{1}{2}$ million years ago) other types of early zebras evolved from the same stock, which seem to resemble *Hippotigris* rather than *Dolichohippus*. It is really remarkable, therefore, that so early on we find the two subgenera of zebras already separate; and, just as remarkable, they evolved in North America! It has been estimated that the environment in which they lived was similar to the more fertile parts of present-day Africa; they survived in North America until the environment changed, perhaps 1 million years ago. In the meantime they had spread their range across the Bering Strait into Eurasia.

Zebras were widespread throughout Europe about 3 million years ago, and continued to be so until 100,000 years ago. Most of the remains can be referred to two species, *Equus stenonis* and *Equus robustus*. *Equus stenonis* was the size of an average modern horse or zebra, 135–45cm high, the earlier races being larger than the later ones, and it has been found in abundance at fossil sites in Italy and southern France. *Equus robustus* was much larger, bigger than the modern Grévy's zebra, and had a more northerly distribution; its remains are found in the Red Crags of East Anglia, and it seemingly overlapped with *Equus stenonis* in France. It was identical to one of the North American species, the so-called *Equus simplicidens*; and it survived in Europe until about 500,000 years ago, evolving into a species called *Equus suessenbornensis* which was found alongside true horses, but, in the increasingly cold climate of Europe, was unable to compete with horses and died out.

In Asia, too, there were big *Dolichohippus* zebras. Both *Equus sanmeniensis* from China and *Equus cautleyi* from India were contemporary with the European zebras, and a similar species named *Equus valeriani* lived in Central Asia as little as 100,000 years ago, where its remains occur alongside those of Neanderthal Man.

All these Eurasian species, like Grévy's zebra, had very elongated narrow skulls with long muzzles, and very thin complex enamel on the cheekteeth. Their skulls had a depression on the side of the muzzle, which some have supposed contained a gland of some sort. Since it is sometimes found in skulls of modern equids without any gland being present, its function is really rather mysterious.

Meanwhile in Africa, zebras directly ancestral to modern species were evolving. At the earliest sites, Makapansgat and Sterkfontein—both perhaps 2½-3 million years old—the only zebra in evidence is *Equus plicatus*, which hardly differs from Grévy's zebra in its known parts; at later sites other species, ancestral to quaggas, mountain zebras and Burchell's zebras, occur as well. Mountain zebra and quagga remains have never been found outside Southern Africa, but Burchell's zebra rapidly spread all over Africa, and was even found until recently—Neolithic times, perhaps—in Algeria. Probably its expansion caused the range of Grévy's zebra to shrink, so that today it is found only in northeast Africa; while the gradually drying-up of the Sahara pushed Burchell's zebra, in turn, back south and it was easily displaced in Algeria by the African wild ass. How the *Hippotigris* zebras arrived in Africa is still a mystery. They appeared in Pliocene North America alongside Grévy-like species, and again in Pleistocene Africa, but their passage across Eurasia is so far unrecorded.

The story of zebras is then quite clear: *Dolichohippus* and *Hippotigris* became separate in North America; both extended their ranges into the Old World, where the former was widespread until recently, while the latter was soon restricted to Africa, where the three living species diversified. What of horses and asses?

THE EMERGENCE OF HORSES AND ASSES

Until recently, the origin of horses was a puzzle. It was assumed that they evolved in Eurasia, since no remains earlier than about 700,000 years old are known from North America, whereas in

Europe a fully-fledged horse, *Equus mosbachensis*, occurs possibly earlier than that; and that it may have evolved from *Equus robustus*. But it has become clear that horses—and asses too—have more in common with *Hippotigris* than with *Dolichohippus*, and so are unlikely to have evolved from *Equus robustus*. It is more probable that they are descended from one of the North American zebras that spread its range to Africa to become the Burchell's/mountain zebra/quagga group. A few years ago a handful of very probably non-zebra teeth were found at a site called Beresti in Moldavia, Rumania. They were described by Radulesco and Samson as a definite horse, *Equus simionescui*. How old the site of Beresti is, we do not know: but certainly it is contemporary with *Equus stenonis* and *Equus robustus*, perhaps 1½–2 million years old. The site of Oltenie, also in Moldavia, has turned up the remains of another somewhat less ancient horse, *Equus aluticus*. Thus the horse line of descent can be traced back more than a million years earlier than *Equus mosbachensis*, and it looks as if the horses of North America represent a migration back into the old equid homeland from Eurasia. *Equus scotti*, a very large heavy horse, lived in the fertile valleys of North America until about 8,000 years ago, and other species spread into the New World from time to time but did not survive so long.

The earliest ass now known is *Equus stehlini* from the site of Val d'Arno in northern Italy, about 1½ million years old: a site where *Equus stenonis* also occurs. It is probably closer to the horse line than to any of the zebras; the same can be said of the very recently described *Equus tabeti* from Algeria. Remains of *Equus sivalensis* from the Siwalik Hills, northern India, show that the onagers had become separate from the African wild asses more than half a million years ago. Asses are also known from contemporary deposits in the southern United States and Mexico: *Equus conversidens* being the best-known species. It is probably at least as closely related to onagers as to the African wild ass.

A word must finally be said about some members of the genus *Equus* which failed to make it into the modern world. These species, zebra-like in their skulls but with distinctive teeth, are placed in a separate subgenus, *Amerhippus*. Two species found in North America, *Equus fraternus* and *Equus occidentalis*, both of them rather late in time—indeed, the latter may have died out in early historic times—were rather distinct from other North American equids; one of them entered South America, where its remains, classed as a number of distinct species, *Equus andium* and its relatives, occur until early historic times, on the pampas of Argentina. They all had short, broad limbs with a short neck, and like many Burchell's zebras they all lacked the infundibulum of the lower incisors.

Why did equids die out in North and South America? We simply do not know. It is not beyond the bounds of possibility that one of the later species of horse in North America survived to become the nucleus of today's mustangs, but these are certainly mainly descended from escaped domestic stock. And it is quite out of the question that the wild horses of the pampas today are derived from *Equus andium*, for the latter was essentially a zebra.

So the first split between the subgenera of *Equus* was between *Dolichohippus* and *Hippotigris*, and horses and asses are derived from the latter. This means that the earliest members of the genus were almost certainly striped. It would be difficult, however, to reconstruct the pattern; for although there are many similarities between the stripe patterns of Grévy's zebra and the *Hippotigris* zebras—black on white banding, tendency for the belly to remain unstriped, dark coloured muzzle, striped mane—there are many differences too, and we cannot easily extrapolate back to a mixture of the patterns seen in today's species. But the existence of stripes, and their progressive reduction in asses and horses, is certain enough. Also, characters which distantly related equids share, can be reasonably supposed to be 'left over' from the ancestral characters: such as the tufted tail, and the presence of chestnuts on the forelimbs only. This makes the subgenus *Equus*, the horse itself, with its fully haired tail and hindlimb chestnuts, the most highly evolved in many ways of the living equids.

2 Wild Horses

INTRODUCING THE PRZEWALSKI HORSE

We walked up the hill to the top of the zoo. Looking down, the city of Prague was spread out before us. As we turned towards the several large grass and mud paddocks on the hilltop, a camel ambled away from the fence of one of them and walked down towards the little knot of wild asses grazing, as far away as possible from the fence, in the middle of the field. We hauled ourselves over the fence and walked down the field; the wild asses moved well out of our way before we were anywhere near them, determinedly but unhurriedly. When we reached the bottom of the sloping paddock we climbed another fence and into the enclosure next door; the field was empty, all its occupants must be indoors.

Rounding the shed we saw them. At first glance they looked like ordinary horses but on closer inspection there were obvious differences. For one thing they were reddish, even orange, in colour. Their colour pattern was distinctive: light muzzles, narrow white rings round the eyes, dark stripes along their backs. Their manes were short and brush-like and stood stiff rather than falling to one side. They did not have long hairs starting from the root of the tail; on the contrary, their tails were initially short-haired with the dorsal stripe continuing on to them. The longer hairs began some way down, nearer to the root on the left- and

right-hand side than on the upper side. This then is the Przewalski horse, the wild horse of Mongolia, the last of the true
wild horses. And the Prague herd is the largest herd in the
world.

Vratislav Mazák beamed as he walked up to them. Stable girls
were there, feeding and grooming the horses, and he exchanged
a few words with them, then turned to me. 'This is Uran,' he
said, indicating the big stallion, 'he is the leader of the herd.'
Uran was the only adult male in the group; there were others,
with their own females, in different enclosures, but he was the
stallion who had quickly proved himself the master, and who had
earmarked most of the females.

The majority of the herd were fairly true to type, but one or
two horses were a little different, with manes which tended to
droop over to one side, muzzle less distinctly light-coloured, and
less heavy and chunky heads. These, as Vratislav explained, are
the price one has to pay for a rather unfortunate decision made
early this century. Between 1898 and 1903, Frederic von Falz-
Fein imported over 50 Przewalski foals into Europe, for his new
park at Askania Nova in the Ukraine. Many of these died in
transit, and the methods used by their captors—usually involving
shooting the mother, or the herd stallion, or both—certainly re-
sulted in the death of many more animals than were captured.
Only 11 foals ended up in Askania Nova, partly because of the
high death-rate, but partly also because Carl Hagenbeck, the
director of Hamburg zoo, was bent on breaking Falz-Fein's
monopoly. He sent his agents to Biisk, the collecting station in
Central Asia where the foals were brought prior to sending them
to Europe, outbid Falz-Fein, and bought 28 foals for Hamburg.
These arrived in November 1901. Of all the captured foals, only
8 survived to form the ancestors of the Przewalski horses alive
today. The Askania Nova horses were, alas, totally destroyed
during World War II, but the stock had meantime been dispersed
to other centres, notably Munich. The Hamburg line was also

dispersed, Prague acquiring the largest share, and since the war Prague has been the centre of Przewalski breeding. But the Hamburg line was impure—indeed, Falz-Fein had the last laugh. One of the foals so cunningly snatched by Hagenbeck was not a pure Przewalski: its mother had been a domestic Mongol pony!

The ironic fact is that the wretched hybrid proved more fertile than almost all the other, pure-bred, Przewalskis. Looking at the photos of some of the foals, newly caught, bedraggled, or just arrived at Biisk, some people have opined that they, too, might not be pure-bred. Certainly there was a lot of variation among them; according to their captors, this was because they were caught at three different localities, where three different colour-types were to be found. The late Erna Mohr, the world authority on these and other equids, was inclined to doubt whether the geographic variation was as real as had been claimed, but equally she felt as satisfied as one reasonably could be that the Biisk foals, except for the known cross-bred, were relatively unmixed Przewalskis.

Ever since it received its herd, Prague has been plagued with throwbacks; animals in which the Mongol pony's genes have re-asserted themselves. The Munich line—most of whose stock is now in the Catskill Game Park, in New York State—are not descended from the hybrid, and by and large all conform to type. Therefore, the Prague group have now definitely decided to undertake a programme of selective breeding by weeding out individuals that do not conform to standard. They have been helped in this by the purchase of a young stallion named 'Bars' from Askania Nova: the offspring of Robert Orlik—himself a pure-bred stallion of the Munich line—with Orlitsa, a mare caught in the wild in 1947. Apart from the original captures at the turn of the century, Orlitsa is the only Przewalski horse to be caught in the wild; and from what we hear, she is likely to be the last there will be.

Page 53 (above) *The last of its kind: the Syrian wild ass,* Equus hemionus hemippus, *that died in Schönbrunn zoo, Vienna, in 1929;* (below) *Nubian wild ass,* Equus africanus africanus, *in Catskill Game Park, New York State. This was bred in Munich zoo from a stock imported from northern Eritrea by Heck in 1937*

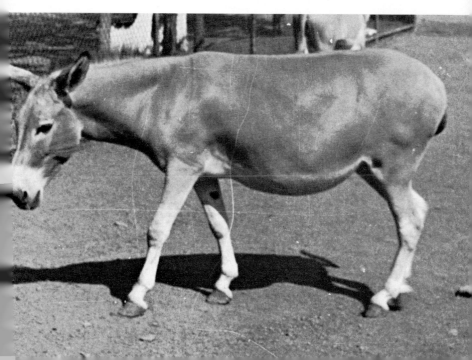

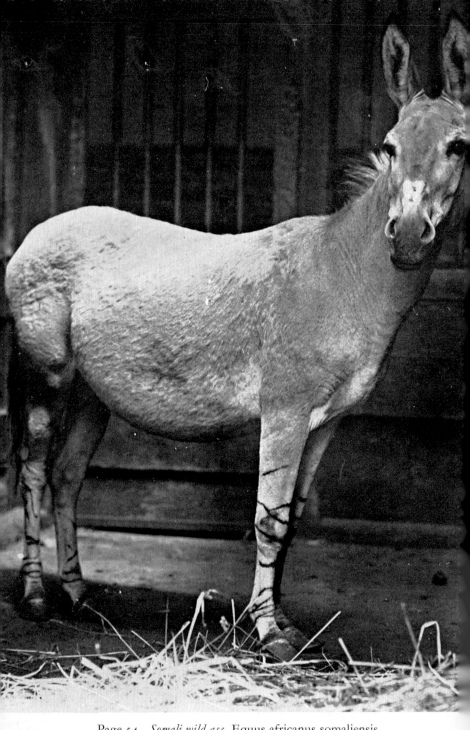

Page 54 *Somali wild ass*, Equus africanus somaliensis

Characteristics of the Przewalski horse

If the Prague group intend to keep to some standard, how will
that standard be determined? And what should it be? Vratislav
Mazák and Ludek Dobroruka, the two Czech horse experts,
have sifted through the evidence, and pointed to certain animals
we can be sure are pure-bred, if any are: the original 'type specimen', the animal shot by Col Przewalski himself in the 1870s,
from which the species *Equus przewalskii* was first described;
other animals shot in the wild, of which pictures have come down
to us, or the skins have been preserved; and, of course, Orlitsa.
The following picture of the 'pure-bred Przewalski horse', that
they have arrived at, will be borne in mind in the course of the
selective breeding at Prague.

The stallion has a height of 138–46cm, the mare of 134–40cm
and the usual weight is 250–300kg. The build is low and robust
with a very strong, relatively short neck; the withers are not
prominent; and the legs are relatively short and slender. The head
is conical; the forehead only slightly vaulted; and the upper and
lower profile lines are straight, with an angle between them of
only 16–20° (in domestic horses, the two profile lines converge
more strongly, the head being less oblong and more triangular,
and the angle between the profile lines is 25–32°). The snout
region is thus much thicker than a domestic horse, the lower
jaw is not concave; and the head is relatively large.

There are two colour-types, both of which can be safely
characterised as pure-bred: one is a light, livid grey-yellow, the
other darker—a lively yellowish red-brown. The foreparts,
especially the neck, are clearly darker than the rest of the body.
The muzzle is light coloured, even white, and there is also a light
narrow ring round the eyes. The lips, the area between the
nostrils and the borders of the nostrils themselves, are very often
black, and contrast strongly with the muzzle. The undersides
are somewhat lighter than the general body colour, but the lower

segments of the limbs—the shanks—are very dark, often black, grading at or above the knees and hocks into the overall body colour. There is a dark to black dorsal stripe, which begins at the back of the mane and runs down the middle of the back and on to the tail; in foals, it may be indistinct especially in winter. The legs show indistinct transverse stripes, which are most clearly expressed on the backs of the knees of the forelegs. There is a very indistinct stripe across the shoulders, usually only a little darker than the rest of the body.

In winter, the coat grows quite long, even shaggy; the hairs can reach a length of 5–8cm on the throat, and on the cheeks and underside of the jaw there is a distinct beard in winter. The mane, which is dark brown to black, is 16–20cm high. It begins between the ears and reaches the withers, and is more or less upright except when slightly tilted to one side in stallions. On either side of the mane, in winter coat, there is a seam of lighter hairs which reach up to about two-thirds of its height. There is no forelock unlike domestic horses.

Most of the basal half of the tail is covered with short hairs and the normal body colour and dorsal stripe are continued on to them. The sides of most of this basal part, and the entire end half of the tail have much longer, stiffer hairs; towards the base these are light-coloured and only on the latter half of the tail are they black. The tail hairs reach to the fetlocks.

Present status

At the time of its discovery, and certainly at least up to the turn of the century, the Przewalski horse was found over a fairly wide area of the western and northern borders of the Gobi desert; certainly from the Dzungarian gates (87° E) across the northern part of Sinkiang to 94° E, and from 44° N as far as the latitude of Kobdo or Jirghalanta, 48° N. Formerly it probably spread further east to Transbaikalia. At the present time, however, there is a doubt whether there are any left in the wild at all. In 1964, Ivor Montagu and Anudarin Dashdorj reported that wild horses probably still existed in Takhin-Shara-nuru—a montane semi-desert country—crossing between Mongolia and China according to season; up to 1963, hunters had from time to time seen small herds of seven or eight. They considered that the animal should survive in the wild, especially as there was a penalty of 5 years' imprisonment for killing one. Since then, however, none have been recorded; a claim by a Hungarian expedition to have sighted a distant herd was refuted when the Prague group, world experts on the Przewalski horse, examined a much enlarged version of the photograph they took, concluding that the animals could as well have been wild asses. It looks very much therefore, as if there are no Przewalski horses remaining in the wild, although it is possible that a few may survive. However, the sole responsibility for the future of the species must lie with those in captivity.

These captives are watched very closely. A studbook has been kept since 1964; the initial data were assembled by Erna Mohr, and since her death in 1969 it has been kept up to date by Jiří Volf of Prague. It is encouraging that, since the book was first entered, every year has shown an increase. In 1964, there were 110 Przewalski horses; as of 1 January 1972, there were 196—an increase of 78 per cent in 8 years, or on average of nearly 10 per cent per annum. The 1972 figures are an increase of 8 per cent over the 1971 figures; there are now 85 males, 111 females, in no fewer than 42 zoos all over the world. In 1971, Prague had 20 horses and Catskill 18; during the course of the year 4 foals were born in each, and one at Catskill died; but Catskill sent four to other zoos, and Prague eight, so that now the Catskill herd is bigger than Prague's. One wonders, in the friendly rivalry between the two breeding centres, which counts for more—having a larger herd, or being a supplier to other institutions?

The original habitat of the Przewalski horse was the saline

high steppe of Mongolia and Dzungaria, between 3,000–4,500ft above sea-level. This stony and sandy semi-desert country on the borders of the Gobi, is dotted with saxaul, tamarisk and worm-wood. Saxaul (*Haloxylon ammonodendron*) is the most characteristic plant which grows in bushes up to 20ft high. Although it is shrubby and dry looking, it does have a very juicy bark.There are also tussock grasses, some up to 6ft high. In summer the steppe is dry and hot; in winter, cold and bleak, with frequent snowstorms. Throughout the year the horses have to go without water sometimes for up to 4 days at a time; in summer, they would dig holes with their hooves, drinking the ground water which was usually salt. They would graze most often in the late evening and early morning, to escape the intolerable heat of the summer sun; during the night, too, some of the desert plants absorb moisture so that an early morning feeding period would be a means of getting more water.

Today their pastures and waterholes have been largely taken over by domestic animals. This underlines the most insidious threat to wild animals today: if land is required for use by expanding human populations, no amount of severe penalties for killing wild animals will save them from extinction. It is no use enacting strict game laws if in the meantime the human population avalanche cuts away the basis for the coexistence of man and wildlife.

The social organisation of the Przewalski horse

The Przewalski herd consists of a stallion and as many as 5 or 6 mares, with offspring of different ages. The herd moves around in single file, the stallion generally in the rear, but in the lead when there seems to be a threat of danger ahead. When the stallion snorts his alarm, the herd flees in single file, the foals in the centre; the stallion stays at the side, or in front or behind, wherever the danger is, even (it was reported) biting the foals to keep them going, or picking one up by the withers and throwing it to help it along. When the herd was cornered the stallion would attack without hesitation; which was why the Falz-Fein captures of the turn of the century involved the shooting of so many herd masters.

Fortunately the essential herd structure seems to be little affected by captivity, especially if the animals are kept in a large paddock. The herd is very cohesive, the stallion circling them and driving them together, head held high, neighing, tail swishing, with an exaggerated trotting gait. He is absolute master of the herd. He keeps himself somewhat apart from the rest of the herd, 25–6oft or more away. His commands are transmitted by movements of his head. When rounding up the mares, he chases them, bites their flanks, then turns and kicks as the mares lash out at him to defend themselves. Often he is so quick at this that the mares have no time to reply. Then he threatens the mares: his ears are laid back, and his head is lowered as he slinks round them. Sometimes the stallion bites too hard and in some captive herds mares have been killed, their entrails torn out.

All this activity emphasises the necessity to keep Przewalski horses in big paddocks. In a small enclosure the male will very likely injure the females, and probably will not cover them. It was found, too, that in large enclosures Przewalski horses will graze peacefully with domestic horses, but in small paddocks they will kill the domestic horses' foals.

When approaching the feeding trough, the mares with foals go first, followed by the older juveniles, then the single mares. The stallion stands aside; at any time, he may move in to eat or drink, and the herd stands back until he has done so, before coming back again.

The coat and its care

Herd cohesiveness is reinforced, as in monkeys, by mutual grooming. The coat of a wild horse is sleek and shiny, and is kept that way by the various grooming procedures which the animals use.

These clean the coat, rid it of ectoparasites, help to loosen hairs during the moulting period, and so on, as well as having their own special part to play in maintaining herd structure. The most basic form of grooming is a simple flicking of the skin by muscle movements. Other methods involve shaking the body to rid it of water or insects, with the horse standing with legs apart and neck stretched forwards; or a sudden flicking of the head, tail or hooves, which may be so rapid that it kills the annoying insect. Rubbing movements, of the head against the legs, or using the hind hooves to scratch the head, are common; but a movement commonly seen among zebras, scratching one hindleg with the other, is not seen. The head and neck are rubbed against trees and fences; the rump, against fences. Foals scratch their backs against the mother's belly. Like domestic horses, they also love to roll in the dust and mud—essentially, a special form of rubbing. Afterwards, the adults rise with their forelegs first, but foals rise with their hindlegs first, like cows and deer.

But biting is the most highly developed and characteristic form of skin-care. A horse may bite its own body and legs, but usually the activity is carried on between two animals. One approaches another with the 'invitation face', in which the mouth is closed and the upper lip pulled slightly forward; then the two fall to, biting and rubbing each other. They stand counterparallel—alongside, head to tail—each nipping away, pulling out loose hairs to bring up the sheen. They bite on the same side as they stand, each biting the same part of the body as the other.

In summer, the thick winter coat is shed—this is the time when skin-care activities, both solitary and mutual, are most frequent. The exact time of onset appears to depend very much on temperature: in Prague in 1958 the moults began in April, when the temperatures climbed above 6° C (43° F); but in 1959 this temperature was reached in March, and the moults started that much earlier. Shedding begins on the head and neck, then the haunches; it extends to the flanks and the back and front of the legs; and last to shed are the belly and the medial and caudal sides of the legs. The whole moult takes 56-7 days in adults, but 74 days in yearlings. The mane is shed 1½-3 months later than the body, and takes 30-50 days to moult completely. Autumn regrowth begins at the end of September and early October; first the jaws acquire their thick beard, then the chest, belly and shanks. The winter coat is fully grown in by early December.

Foals are born with a short, thick coat of hair; after 6-8 days, this changes to the typical foal 'fleece', which in turn begins to be shed after about 7 weeks. The very short mane of foals grows in longer at this time. This first true moult takes only 30-40 days.

Mating behaviour

An activity which is characteristic of the Perissodactyla is that called by the Germans 'flehmen'. There is no good English translation of this word; it is a kind of 'sniff-tasting', but this is a cumbersome expression. It is particularly associated with urination; one animal sniffs another's urine, then raises its head, tilting its head upwards, and draws its lips back and upwards at the same time wrinkling its nostrils. A horse may stand for half a minute in this position. The male always does this when he smells urine; and in the rutting season this is a pretty constant activity with him. Mares do it, too, on greeting each other; even foals sometimes do it. What does it mean?

Undoubtedly, the 'flehm'-ing individual is smelling the other's urine; a male in rut, indeed, may actually thrust his nose into the female's stream of urine. The pulling back of the upper lip probably brings into play an accessory olfactory zone called Jacobson's organ, whose entrance ducts are in the roof of the mouth at the front. Since this organ is not functional in man, it is unknown whether it can detect substances which the nose cannot. The urine of a female in oestrus—ready for mating—contains much oestrogen (the female hormone) and it may be this which the male is trying to detect. Flehmen may be performed outside of oestrus, too; in this case it seems to have become a simple greeting ritual, performed among mares too.

It is at the time of the rut that the stallion becomes most restless and energetic as he constantly rounds up and disciplines the herd, and prepares to defend it against other stallions. Solitary stallions, wandering alone—mostly, one supposes, young males that have left their herds on maturing—would apparently try to gain possession of mares at this time, so that the herd stallions must be on their guard. Probably, even other herd leaders would not be entirely trustworthy at this time: the more females a stallion could cover, the more offspring he can sire. Stallions threaten each other in exactly the same way as a stallion threatens a mare, with his ears laid back and his head lowered, rapidly circling his opponent, each trying to catch the other off guard with his teeth to bring him down. The severe biting matches of rutting stallions are dramatic enough in captivity, and must have been terrifying sights in the wild; that they were lethal, and could result in severe wounds or even death if the loser had no opportunity to get away, seems to contrast sharply with the rutting fights of most other large animals, such as stags, which aim to wrestle the opponent into submission but not to kill him.

A mare on heat not only has a high oestrogen level in her urine; she twitches her tail or holds it stiffly behind her, and shows a restlessness not much less than the male's. If not entirely ready to mate, she may refuse the male with shrill squeals, and it is at such times that, if kept in a small enclosure, she stands a risk of being injured by him. The male does not mount his own fillies, nor others that have grown up with his herd.

Mares and their foals

The mare drops her foal in a quiet place, returning about 9 days later to the herd. Birth takes place at night. Gestation averages

335 days, about 11 months, so that foals are born just before the new rut. As soon as the female returns to the herd with her new foal she comes into oestrus again. Przewalski horses seem to preserve considerable seasonality in their breeding; at Askania Nova, 48 per cent of all births have taken place in May with another 16 per cent each in April and June, and even in the much less severely seasonal climate of Prague, 37½ per cent of all births have been in May, with 17½ per cent and 20 per cent respectively in April and June. Interestingly enough, of 5 foals born in the southern hemisphere (in Sydney), only one has been born in May—the other four, in September! Obviously the animals altered their internal clocks to adjust to the reversed seasons.

When the foal is born, the mother removes the caul with her teeth but does not eat it, unlike many antelopes. The foals suckle for brief periods of 45–60 seconds at a time. They follow their mothers, gradually being weaned on to hard food, over a period of 2 years. Like most other hoofed animals, they can get up in their first hour of life, and soon begin to run about. They play, running and prancing, alone and with other foals, and also with other mares, especially barren ones; but mares often take a dislike to strange foals, kicking and chasing them away. Nor does the stallion play with his foals, unlike the leader of a herd of cattle. Foals will become as tame as a domestic horse if handled from an early age, but are taught to fear man by their mothers. The story is told of a foal at Halle zoo which willingly let itself be stroked and petted until its mother let out a warning squeal, when at once its temper changed and it bucked and kicked. And so it is that even captive-bred Przewalski horses (which means, of course, all of them except for Orlitsa) are skittish. They can be calmed and handled safely, and at Prague Vratislav Mazák and I entered their paddock, although sudden movements and harassment could have destroyed a carefully nurtured situation. Mares strenuously defend their foals, kicking back at potential aggressors with their hind hooves, with a jet of urine which is sprayed about by the underside of the hooves.

Most stallions breed for the first time in their fifth year, but some in captivity have bred for the first time at 3 years; mares usually breed at the beginning of their fourth year. The record upper age for breeding in a mare is 24, and several have produced young at over 20 years of age; the record number of foals for one mare is 13—an average of almost one a year, if we assume the first at 5 years and the last at about 20.

Males, as in many mammals, are subject to greater lethal stresses than females, and especially in the second year of life there is a high death rate—even in captivity. This goes a long way to explaining the very uneven sex ratio of adults; the 1:4 or 5 male/female ratio in the herds is by no means evened up by the existence of a number of young stallions living a solitary life. Even in the high-survival conditions of captivity, the sex ratio of all ages is 85:111.

Males do, however, go on breeding for a longer period than females; one male is known to have sired a foal at age 31. Normally, Przewalski horses do not live much beyond 20–5 years, although the maximum so far has been 34. The same average age is reached in domestic horses, but here—as with most mammals —a few exceptionally long-lived individuals are encountered: the maximum appears to be 61 years, and three horses are said to have lived to 49.

The birth weight of a foal is 25–30kg; this doubles in 4 weeks and, as in man and most other mammals the youngster grows with continually decreasing velocity until it reaches full size. This is reached at about 4 years for mares, 6–7 years for stallions.

The stallion's role

The dominant male in the herd has a heavy physical and psychological burden on him. L. J. Dobroruka, formerly of Prague zoo, has brought this out by calculating how much of each animal's time is spent in different activities: feeding, locomotion, sleeping. He found that the two dominant males he watched spent 25–45 per cent of their time in locomotion, whereas other herd members spent under 10 per cent in this activity. The stallions were therefore more continuously restless and alert. Only 5–6 per cent of their time was spent asleep, compared to 20–7 per cent for others, although the two mothers of week-old foals also did not sleep much: the foals themselves slept for about half of the 24 hours. The two mothers spent 70–85 per cent of their time feeding, which is understandable since the drain on an animal of lactation is extremely high; the others also spent over half their time in feeding—the young males up to 70 per cent, the young females less, the dominant males less still. Already at this stage the foals were feeding on solid food for a longer time (7–15 per cent) than they spent in suckling (4–7 per cent).

The stallion is not the only herd member with a special position. The leading mare also seems to have an important function to perform, it seems to be her role to determine the time and direction of daily movement. Many of the behaviours of the other herd members are directed to her, not to the stallion. We shall see later that in other equids mare-leadership is the rule, so that an arrangement of this nature in Przewalski horses, where the stallion is not an integral member of the herd in the fullest sense, is not surprising.

Vocalisations

Przewalski horses have a variety of vocalisations. As in man, both visual communication, in the form of body postures, facial gestures, ear positions and so on, and auditory communication are important. Like a domestic horse, the Przewalski horse neighs: to be interpreted, by and large, as indicating a wish for (or expectation of) food, water, or the company of other horses. A rutting stallion utters a laugh-like grunt towards a mare in heat, or a rival stallion separated from him by a fence; this may be punctuated by a squeal as he paws the ground or rears up. A mare squeals if she refuses the stallion, or when she defends her foal from an enemy, and as she does this her ears are laid and her tail tucked in, ready to lash out with her hooves. A neighing horse pricks his ears forward; the laughing-squealing stallion moves his ears to and fro, lashing his flanks with his tail.

THE TARPAN

The Przewalski horse is not the only wild horse to have existed in historic times. Although we have very few specimens, the evidence is that almost until the present day there existed on the steppes of European Russia a mouse-grey wild horse, the tarpan. The first detailed description was given by the naturalist Gmelin, who found them in the spring of 1769 near Voronesh. He described the tarpans as being 'hardly as large as the smallest Russian horses'. The head was very thick, the ears pointed and often long like an ass's; the mane was short and frizzy; and the tail covered with hair, 'but always somewhat shorter than in tame horses'. All the wild horses in that district were mouse-coloured, the belly ash-grey, the shanks black. The hair, he said, was very long and thick. They ran very fast, were extremely frightened of noise, and their herds were led by a stallion who had a defensive role. The stallion abducted tame mares and was known to kill the domestic stallion in the process. They were difficult to tame.

The work of the Russian zoologist Heptner, the Polish scientist Pruski and others has established just how the tarpan differed from the Przewalski horse. It was smaller, only 130cm high, and had smaller teeth; the snout was less thick, with a depression in the mid-nasal region giving it a dished face; the muzzle was not light-coloured, and the general body-colour was mouse-grey instead of rufous. Like the Przewalski horse, however, the basal half of the tail seems to have been short-haired; the shanks were blackish; and there was a dark stripe running along the back. Opinions differ about the mane: Gmelin described it as 'short and frizzy', which has generally been taken to mean that it stood upright like a Przewalski horse's, but need not mean this at all; a photograph published by W. Pruski, of a tarpan that died in Moscow zoo in 1887, shows a mane that is short but none the less falls to one side. There is doubt, however, about whether this animal was pure-blooded; doubt, indeed, has been expressed about whether the wild horses of the Russian steppes could be described as pure-blooded in general, since they seem to have abducted tame mares. Pruski records, however, that the wild herds were always said to be led by grey-coloured stallions, never by hybrids which were generally easy to recognise; this in turn would imply that most of the stallions—and probably all of the breeding ones—would have a predominance of wild blood. This, of course, is precisely what one would expect: the characteristics bred into wild horses by generations of natural selection would ensure that the wild stallions were of far superior fitness to animals with a proportion of domestic blood.

Colonel Hamilton Smith, whose travels and natural history writings made many new species known to science in the early half of the last century, was concerned to find out more about wild horses in general and took the opportunity, when in Russia in 1814, of interviewing Cossacks and other non-Russian troops, about them. They told him that the wild horses of eastern Europe were predominantly grey, but with much intermixture of domestic horses, and that the only really unmixed wild horses were to be found towards the borders of China. The purest, they said, were found on Lake Karakorum, south of the Aral Sea, on the Syr Darya river, and in Mongolia. The horses of Central Asia were tan, isabella or mouse-coloured, with a whitish winter surcoat, shed in May.

Other sources, too, spoke of wild horses from Eastern Europe right across to the Chinese border. It seems that at one time the population was continuous, linking up with the Przewalski horses in Mongolia and Dzungaria. On the Ural river in 1762, both red-brown and 'blue' horses were reported, and similarly in the

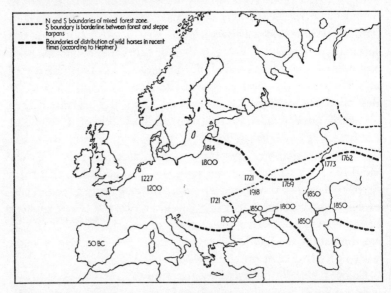

Fig 3 *Distribution of tarpans* (Equus ferus *subspecies*) *in Europe during historical times. The dates indicate the last records of wild horses in a particular area*

early nineteenth century east of the Volga near Saratov. Heptner has suggested, plausibly, that this was in an intergrade zone between the true tarpan and the Przewalski horse: west of the Volga, the 'blue' (mouse-grey) tarpan, east of the Ural the reddish Przewalski horse, and between the two rivers a hybrid population. If this is so, it means that the two types of wild horse must have been geographic variants—subspecies—of the same species, since there was no reproductive isolation between them.

Otto Antonius, in 1912, gave the name *Equus gmelini* to the type of wild horse depicted by these early descriptions. But much earlier, in 1785, Boddaert had, on the basis largely of Gmelin's description, erected a species *Equus ferus*. This much earlier name is the one that must therefore be used for this species of wild horse; it seems that the European tarpan should be called *Equus ferus ferus* (as the 'nominate', or first-described, race of the species), while the Przewalski horse, described for the first time by Poliakov in 1881, must be called *Equus ferus przewalski*.

Forest tarpans

But other wild horses certainly existed both in Europe and in Asia in historic times, and probably belonged to yet other distinct races. Herodotus (484–25 BC) described white wild horses living in marshy country in northern Europe; Pliny (AD 23–79) also mentioned wild horses in northern Europe, probably like those seen by Herodotus, in Poland and the southern Baltic region; and Varro (116–27 BC) described wild horses in Spain. In the *Niebelunglied*, written c AD 1200, Siegfried slew a 'fierce Schelch', a wild horse, in the neighbourhood of Worms. In 1227 they were patrolling croplands in the Moselle region to protect them from wild horses. The last tarpan outside Russia was killed at Königsberg, Lithuania, in 1814. Gabriel Rzaczynski (1665–1730) had described wild horses here around 1721, as well as in Byelorussia, the Carpathians, and the Ukrainian plains around Borysthenum; and we have good descriptions of tarpans in the Caucasus up until the latter half of the nineteenth century, when they were exterminated.

As the steppes were ploughed up, and domestic animals competed with wild horses for the grazing that remained, the tarpans were pushed back and back. The last remaining one died in 1918 on an estate in Dubrowka, Poltava district, in the Ukraine.

Certainly, the wild horses to the north-west of the Ukrainian steppes lived in forest not on the plains. To judge from descriptions, and from the appearance of their domestic descendants—the *konik* ponies of the Polish peasantry—they were a little smaller than the steppe tarpans and they became very light coloured, almost white, in winter. They have been set apart as a distinct subspecies, *Equus ferus sylvaticus*, by Vetulani based more on supposition and reconstruction than on actual specimens; in the 1820s however, the still-existing forest tarpans of Bialowiecz had been given the name *Equus ferus sylvestris* by von Brincken. The validity is not firmly established, and no really detailed description of a wild one to compare with Gmelin's description or the photos of steppe tarpans exists; but the probability is high that the konik is a nearly pure-bred descendant of this form, whereas no direct, unmixed descendant of the steppe tarpan exists. The last forest tarpans, captured in the Bialowiecz forest of Poland in the early years of the last century, were kept for a time in a zoo at Samosch; then, because their numbers increased unmanageably, some were shot; some were used for Roman-type combats with carnivores; and the remainder were divided among the peasants in the Bilgoraj district. The Polish authorities have recently purchased a number of koniks and bred from them selectively, so that today, once again, the forest tarpan roams through the open glades of Bialowiecz.

Recreating the tarpan

It is rather more difficult to reconstitute the steppe tarpan, as no domestic breeds are directly descended from it. Ukrainian ponies certainly contain a lot of tarpan blood, but which others do is open to question. The Heck brothers, directors of Berlin and Munich zoos before the war (Heinz Heck still directs Munich

Page 71 (above) *A very rare animal: the Cape mountain zebra,* Equus zebra zebra. *This female was photographed in Stellingen zoo, Hamburg, 1917;* (below) *Hartmann's mountain zebra,* Equus zebra hartmannae, *in the Kaokoveld of South-West Africa (Namibia)*

Page 72   (above) *The quagga,* Equus quagga. *This species was abundant in Cape Province and the Orange Free State in the early nineteenth century, but by about 1870 when this was taken, it was extinct in the wild;* (below) *a herd of Damara zebras,* Equus burchelli antiquorum, *at Etosha Pan, South-West Africa* (Namibia)

zoo), decided to try to breed back the steppe tarpan in the same way that they had reconstituted the appearance of the aurochs, the primeval European wild bull. Their choice of initial breeding stock, however, is distinctly questionable; and so, I think, was their idea of what the steppe tarpan looked like. Heinz Heck put Icelandic ponies and Gotland horses together, these being the two breeds he considered most like the tarpan; he then selected those offspring with a greyish colour and a dorsal stripe, and mated them with Przewalski horses to obtain an erect mane. We have already seen that it is by no means settled that the tarpan did have an erect mane; and we shall see later on that Gotland horses probably have no tarpan ancestry, and Icelandic ponies very little. In pre-war days it was taken for granted that the tarpan was 'the' ancestor of all domestic horses, so the Heck brothers can hardly be blamed for selecting what to them appeared to be the breeds which most closely resemble a primitive wild horse.

The Heck tarpans are, all the same, fairly plausible looking animals: mouse-grey as they should be, with a dorsal stripe and dark shanks, and hard hooves. The mane is more or less erect; the tail, and this seems decidedly wrong, has long hairs growing from the root. Lutz Heck's tarpans were destroyed during World War II; Heinz Heck's may still be seen in Munich zoo, at Catskill and at Brookfield zoo, Chicago. An unexpected feature is that the foals are born with foxy-red overtones, changing colour as they grow up. Heptner is of the opinion that the tarpan may have done that in any case: so once again, the Heck brothers may not have been so wide of the mark.

OTHER WILD HORSES

What of Herodotus's 'white horse'? We have seen that forest tarpans did, in fact, turn nearly white in winter, and the marshes that Herodotus spoke of were, it has been suggested, the extensive

Pripet Marshes in Byelorussia, on the edges of the Bialowiecz forest. There is, however, another white wild horse that has been recorded: not, almost certainly, the one mentioned by Herodotus, but a most exciting report all the same.

The remarkable explorer Pfizenmayr led an expedition in 1901 into the Siberian tundra to look for mammoths. Mammoth carcasses are from time to time frozen whole in the permafrost, and as the ice gradually melts they rear up grotesquely out of the ground. Ivory of any kind is valuable, and this—rather than any directly scientific purpose—was the object of the expedition. In his book, *Siberian Man and Mammoth*, published in 1939, Pfizenmayr tells how two Lamuts told him that wild horses lived in their country—along the Omolon river, between Omolon and Anjui in the Kolyma basin. They were of similar size to the Yakut domestic horse—that is, a little larger than the Przewalski horse—with long, whitish-grey hair and a fatty, pleasant-tasting flesh. Later, an exiled Russian student in Verkhoyansk told him that in the northern part of that district an ivory hunter had found the carcass of a horse, sticking out of frozen earth in a fissure in the bank of a frozen lake; this carcass had long greyish-white hair. In this latter area, which is about 400 miles west of the Lamut district, there were then no settlements 'for hundreds of miles'. One can therefore presume that these were not the remains of a domestic horse.

What makes all this especially interesting is that subfossil remains of wild horses have been discovered at several places in northern Siberia. Though at first assigned to the Upper Pleistocene, these skulls and limb bones are probably more recent than that, since the sites where most of them were found, on the New Siberian Isles, were glaciated during the last Ice Age and so would have been uninhabitable. However, a frozen carcass from the River Garyn has been dated at 37,000 years old. At sites along the Yana river, in the northern Verkhoyansk district, remains of two types of horse have turned up; but at the other sites—Kotielny and Liakhov islands, and Khatanga on the Taimyr peninsula—only one type of horse, corresponding to the smaller Yana type, was discovered. The zoologist Brauner, in 1936, gave the smaller type the name *Equus tscherskii*, after the palaeontologist Tscherski who in the 1870s described the Liakhov skull. The skulls are basically similar to those of tarpans and Przewalski horses, but have a shorter snout—in fact, a very short snout indeed—and their teeth are small like those of the tarpan. The type of horse they represented, to judge from the remains, would have stood about 140cm high.

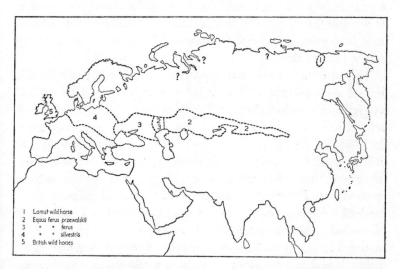

1 Lomut wild horse
2 Equus ferus przewalskii
3 "   "   ferus
4 "   "   silvestris
5 British wild horses

Fig 4 *Known distribution in postglacial times of the races of* Equus ferus

But the story does not end there. An American palaeontologist, Oliver Hay, in 1913 described a complete skull of a horse dug up in the Tofty mining district of Alaska, under the name *Equus niobrarensis alaskae* (he thought it was related to *Equus niobrarensis*, which he had described earlier from the Middle Pleistocene of Nebraska; but it has nothing to do with it, since this latter is probably a variant of the heavy-limbed *Equus scotti*, described in Chapter 1). The Alaskan skull is almost identical to the Liakhov one: they might be brothers! In 1917, Hay described another horse from Alaska, which he dubbed *Equus lambei*, which is considerably smaller than the Tofty skull. Later on still he referred a skull to the same species, which is intermediate in size and shape; obviously, all three belong to the same type. We do not know what colour the Alaskan horses were, but from the total identity of their skulls with those of the Siberian horses, it would simply be illogical to keep them separate. We have therefore a tundra race of wild horse, from both the Old and New World tundra zones; the prior name for it would be *Equus ferus alaskae*. It lived in the Upper Pleistocene but may well have survived, at least in Siberia, into recent times; and if Pfizenmayr was right, up to the present day.

The other recent evidence consists not of reports, nor of bones, but of rock-paintings. The Saharan peoples who painted and engraved the rock-shelters of Tibesti, Fezzan, Ennedi and Tassili left remarkable records of the fauna amongst which they lived. In their day the Sahara, or at least most of it, was not so arid as it is now, and comprised open savannah, with elephants, giraffes, hartebeest and white rhinoceroses. Horses, too, appear in their rock-art. At Ennedi, for example, there is a rock-painting of an undoubted horse—not an ass or a zebra—which has been much discussed. Ebhardt dated it at 8000 BC, but Brentjes, an international authority on African rock-art, is more inclined on stylistic grounds to date it at 1400–1200 BC, so it might well be a representation of a domestic horse. The Hyksos invaders of Egypt (c 1600 BC) are currently considered to have been the agents of the introduction of the horse to Africa, so any picture from an earlier period would, theoretically, represent a wild horse. Unfortunately we have no evidence from an earlier time, and there is no adequately identified fossil material of North African horses. Thus the whole theory of an indigenous North African wild horse rests on a very insecure basis.

At Nineveh there are depictions of horses also presumed by some to be wild, as they date from the first millenium BC when horses are not known to have been domesticated in Mesopotamia. The horses shown are thin-legged, small-eared, and small-headed like Arabian horses. The Russian palaeontologist Vereschagin has opined that the Nineveh pictures represent the type of wild horse found up to the southern flank of the Caucasus in post-glacial times; but for this type, too, the evidence is extremely dubious.

FERAL HORSES

But what of the other horses and ponies that we call wild? The mustangs of the 'Wild West'; the brumbies of Australia; the wild ponies of the British Isles? When we speak of the Przewalski horse as the 'only true wild horse', what are we implying about these others?

The point is, that all of these are either known to be descended from domestic stock that ran wild, or are suspected to have done so. Many conform to a typical 'standard type', but this is probably because they are basically descended from a single breed of domestic horse, and are influenced by similar survival requirements. This is what is meant by the term feral.

The brumbies of Australia

Perhaps more is known about the history of Australia's wild ponies than any other type, because something of their introduction is on record. We can be certain that there never were any truly wild horses in Australia: the Australian mammals are all either monotremes (egg-laying mammals—the platypus and the echidna), marsupials (pouched mammals—kangaroos, wombats, opossums and so on) or else small mouse-like rodents, or bats.

There are no large, placental mammals: that is, no large mammals like those found over most of the rest of the world. Even the wild dogs, or dingoes, are descended from aborigines' dogs that ran wild.

For some reason the early settlers were not satisfied with the remarkable indigenous fauna: perhaps they were just not used to kangaroo meat, and were not prepared to try. They therefore introduced all kinds of exotic wild animals such as buffaloes, camels, and rabbits. These have all multiplied enormously and played havoc with the marsupials, causing the extermination of some species by competing with them for space and food. More recently, they have begun to compete with domestic animals, especially sheep; and modern Australians have come to deeply regret that their ancestors did not leave things as they were.

The wild horses of the Northern Territory are descended from Timor ponies, which have been breeding wild there for 130 years. Living in small groups, a stallion with 3–4 mares and their foals, these bold and inquisitive animals are up to 120cm high, lightly built, with long manes and tails. They are most often bay or brown, but some grey, chestnut and creamy individuals occur. On the Cobourg peninsula there are some 300; farther inland, towards the centre, there are many more, and they are regularly caught and broken. One station on the Roper river annually traps 300, of which the best are broken—the rest are slaughtered to make pet food.

On the whole these 'brumbies', as they are called, are not popular with stock-breeders. They upset cattle and sheep, eat the same range grass, and disturb and foul the water. Neither are they particularly healthy and attractive specimens: they are heavily parasitised, and often not only succumb to these infestations when captured, but pass them on to domestic horses. For several years up to World War II, Central Australia provided horses for the Indian army, and many escaped to add to the feral stock.

The mustangs of North America

Undoubtedly there were truly wild horses in North America up to about 3,000 years ago; they were hunted by the Indians but not, it seems, domesticated. Why they disappeared we do not know; indeed, it is an attractive theory that perhaps they did not disappear, and that the wild horses of the West contain some of their blood. There is really no evidence for this since no detailed comparisons have been made, but it does seem that wild horses were unknown—at least in the south-west—until after 1541. In that year, Coronado—a companion of Cortez—set out north from Mexico to look for treasure. He had with him 16 horses; on the expedition, they escaped and they formed, so it seems, the nucleus of the wild horse population of North America.

'Mustang', the name by which these horses are usually known, is a corruption of the Spanish *mesteño*, meaning ownerless; they are also known locally as 'broomtails'. By the end of the eighteenth century, they had spread their range from the Rio Grande in the south to the Athabaska river in the north, from the Mississippi river in the east to the Pacific in the west. They numbered, at that time, perhaps between 2 and 6 million, most being concentrated in the south-west (Texas to Colorado). Their number was of course added to by new escapes, and by animals turned loose deliberately, from the very earliest days. Like the Australian brumbies, the American mustangs have never been popular with ranchers; they have been accused of depleting the range, competing with livestock and with big game, and luring away domestic mares to join them.

The fencing of the range restricted the mustang, and gradually it was forced west of the Rockies. Mustangs were shot, poisoned, caught or broken. Although many were caught for use in the Boer War and World War I, in the 1920s only a few were caught, and the professional mustangers worked mainly to supply meat for chicken feed and pet food, and for export for human consumption in the Netherlands, Scandinavia and other parts of Europe. Their numbers declined and they became warier and tougher.

Then the climate of opinion changed. People began to call for their preservation, for although they were not part of the indigenous fauna, they had become part of the 'Wild West' scene. They did after all have their uses: they helped spread seeds in their faeces, break the ice on standing water in the winter and keep the snow trails open—all of these activities helped the ranchers. Today, they are on the increase again—at a rate, so it is claimed, of 30 per cent per annum! Their biographer, Tom McKnight, estimated in 1958 that there were between 17,000 and 33,000 in the United States—of which the largest concentration, 5,000–7,000, is in Nevada. There are also many hundreds in Alberta and British Columbia.

Probably the ancestors of the mustangs were Arab and Barb horses—the breeds used by the Spaniards at that time. The modern mustangs have, by all accounts, lost much of the fineness of their forebears. They are described as ugly, runty, bigheaded, coarse and vicious, but agile and full of stamina. Most do not make good riding horses, which is why the pet food market was so well served by them. But for one group of people they were a godsend. The Indians, making up for their ancestors' failure to domesticate the original American wild horses, not only stole horses from settlers but even learned to break and ride the mustangs, and used the wild herds as a source of fresh domestic stock. In a remarkably short space of time a whole culture, the Plains Indians' war-culture, grew up based entirely on the horse; and several breeds, such as the Appaloosa and Palomino, arose during that time.

Other feral horses

Like North America, South America too had its indigenous wild horses: not, this time, variants of more widespread Old World species, but the curious *Amerhippus* horses. They too are gone today; in their place are feral horses on the Argentine pampas. Like the mustangs, they are regularly caught and broken; like them, they are poor-quality stock said not to be suitable for riding.

In Europe there are a number of breeds of feral horses. Northern Sweden, in mixed tundra and forest country, has herds of dark brown horses with flowing manes and tails. The famous grey horses of the Camargue—the marshy land of the Rhône delta in southern France—are also included in this category. Like the Swedish horses, they have long flowing manes and tails, but are smaller—a little over 120cm high. These strong, hardy horses are derived from Arab stock which ran wild during the Roman occupation of Gaul. Although their origin reaches back thus not much over 2,000 years, they have adapted in that time by developing large feet with hard, flat hooves: enabling the weight to be spread over a wider area of the soft marshy ground. The locals prize them for their strength and swiftness.

Another interesting feral breed is the Haflinger. Large, russet-coloured horses with a light mane and tail, and often with light coloured faces, Haflingers live in the Tyrol, on the slopes of the Otz river valley. These, like several other breeds in Europe, live semi-wild lives, spending most of the time out on the barren hill-sides, occasionally being rounded up to have the best of them broken and trained.

British feral ponies

Nine breeds of semi-wild ponies live in the British Isles: five in England (New Forest, Dartmoor, Exmoor, Dales and Fells), one in Wales (Welsh mountain), two in Scotland (Highland and Shetland) and one in Ireland (Connemara). The largest of these, the Dales breed, stand 145cm at the withers; the smallest, the Shetland, can be as little as 71cm high.

Shetland ponies are known for their great strength as much as for their small size. Indeed, they are stronger in relation to their size, than any other breed. They may be as much as 107cm high, and in any case tend to grow larger in warmer, more fertile climates than in the Shetlands; they have broad chest and hind-quarters, flowing mane and tail, large eyes set wide apart, and small ears; they may be any colour, but black ones are favoured. They have certainly been living a largely wild existence for hundreds of years, and were not extensively bred and their type 'fixed' until Lord Londonderry began a programme of selection between 1870 and 1899. Even today Shetlands mostly live out all year round, only the breeding stallions being taken in sometimes for the winter.

Highland ponies are much more variable in appearance than Shetlands. They can be 127–42cm high, with a range of colours including chestnut with a silvery mane and tail, and may have a dark dorsal stripe and zebra-stripes on the knees and hocks. Like Shetlands they tend to be sturdy with small ears, eyes set wide apart, and a flowing mane and tail. They generally have long hair, or 'feather', round the hooves. Those on the Western Isles are smaller and have a considerable amount of Arab blood; those of the mainland are said to have more French blood, and are stronger and heavier.

It is quite possible that the Highland ponies have a strain of truly wild blood in them; the same may be true for the Connemara breed of Ireland. Certainly the Connemara has a great deal of Arab blood in it; but horse skulls, thought to be early post-glacial, are known from Irish peat-bogs at a time when no domestic horses are thought to have been used in Ireland. The Connemara is found in the hills of Galway; it stands 132–42cm high, may be almost any colour, has a deep compact body and short legs. It is known for its docility. There are very few left in the wild state; most are brought in during the winter, and as they make good jumpers, their breeding is controlled.

The Welsh mountain pony is probably less mixed than the Connemara or Highland breeds; they, too, may have native wild stock in them, although they are certainly descendants of Oriental-type horses left by the Romans. They are sturdily built with a heavy head, a shorter mane and tail than the Scottish breeds, and may be almost any colour. Their herds are technically owned, but may live quite wild. They have long been caught for use by shepherds; in the last century they were employed as pit ponies.

The large, hardy Dales and Fell ponies—strong and sure-footed—resemble miniature cart-horses in their heavy build, long legs, and the silky 'feather' over the fetlocks. Most are brought in during the winter months, although a few Fell ponies still breed wild in the Lake District, in the Haweswater–Ullswater area.

The New Forest ponies are as variable as any of the others, at least in colour: although piebald and skewbald animals are rejected as impure. All are owned, and marked with brands; their breeding is controlled through the selection of stallions, which are caught and shown in April, and those that fall below par are weeded out, the rest allotted districts for the summer. The mares are free year-round; they are very sedentary, living in groups of 1–6 with their offspring, within which there is a stable rank-order. The home ranges of the different groups overlap, but there is no aggression between them. The foals are born in May and June; in autumn they are rounded up (on horseback) and branded, the mares released and the colts retained for sale. The New Forest, in southern Hampshire between the River Avon and Southampton Water, is a crown forest, formerly a royal hunting preserve. The origin of the ponies is unknown; here too there may have been a native wild strain, although it is far from dominant. At any rate, the ponies play a considerable part in keeping the forest relatively open, preventing it from growing thicker and denser.

The Dartmoor ponies are not unlike those of the New Forest.

Here, however, the breeding of stallions is not controlled, so the variability is if anything greater. The typical Dartmoor pony has a small head with tiny ears; is about 120cm high but may be as much as 127cm; and is bay, black or brown, although there are many greys—but piebalds and skewbalds are not found. They are easy to tame, gentle in nature and like most 'wild' ponies, they are owned, and bear their owners' brand.

The last of the British semi-wild breeds is the Exmoor pony. Here at once one realises, is something different. Although there are non-standard ponies on Exmoor, they are recognised as being impure: the true Exmoor type is very uniform. They are dun or brown, with little or no white; they have a light-coloured, so-called 'mealy' muzzle; a wide forehead, prominent eyes, short thick ears (mealy inside); a height of some 127cm; a harsh springy coat, a deep wide chest, and lean limbs. The foals have a woolly undercoat. Their hardiness is well known; it is said that in a hard winter the sheep will succumb first, then the deer, and the ponies last. Although they are privately owned, and rounded up and inspected in October, they essentially live a wild existence. On the moor, the herds are formed by 20–5 mares with a single stallion who herds them and disciplines them like a Przewalski horse. Foals are born in May.

Is it possible that Exmoor ponies are direct descendants of native wild ponies? Formerly dismissed, this theory is now seriously considered by many hippologists, especially Speed (of Edinburgh) and Ebhardt (of Hamburg). Indeed, the latter considers that the Exmoor is the *only* pure-blooded wild horse: even the Przewalski horse, he holds, is a cross-bred! We will discuss Ebhardt's theories in Chapter 5; in the meantime, it must be agreed that the possibility is intriguing and has much to recommend it, since Exmoor-like ponies with mealy muzzles and foal undercoats turn up from time to time in the other feral breeds. For example, there is a typical Exmoor herd on the Pentland Hills, near Edinburgh. The Exmoor Crown 'forest' was known as the home of wild ponies from time immemorial. Furthermore, this part of Britain was never glaciated, and in the Mendip Caves, in deposits going back perhaps 100,000 years, remains indistinguishable from Exmoor ponies have been discovered. Elsewhere in Britain, remains of similar type have been found in Aveline's Hole, Burrington, dated at 10,000–8,000 BC.

One could conclude from this evidence that, alongside the Przewalski horse (assuming that this *is* a pure type), the tarpan, and the Lamut wild horse, we must place the British wild pony as an aboriginal type; and that this type, while it comes out at times in many feral breeds, has survived in purest form in the ancient wild ponies of Exmoor.

3 Wild Asses

THE KIANG

Habitat

The hot, densely packed plains and river valleys of peninsular India have little remaining wildlife. Fifteen hundred tigers, seven hundred rhinos, a few thousand elephants: the pathetic remnants of a once teeming wilderness now hide away in odd unwanted corners, wherever man has left space for them.

North of the flatlands of the peninsula lies a different world. The land becomes undulating; here and there we can still find forests. The Ganges valley has given way to the foothills and mountains: the dreaming valleys of Kashmir, and the mountain kingdoms of Nepal, Sikkhim and Bhutan. On their northern borders, the land rises higher than it does anywhere else on earth, forming a jagged barrier 1,000 miles long, reaching up to $5\frac{3}{4}$ miles high at its highest point. Beyond this mountain chain, the land drops again, but only to 13,000ft—for behind the Himalayas lies Tibet, the roof of the world.

The wildlife of Tibet is mainly a southern extension of the northern temperate zone fauna. Some mammals, like the wolf, corsac fox, brown bear, lynx, goral, red deer, roe deer, pika, marmot and souslik, are local races of species which have extended up on to the plateau from their main areas of distribution in the forests of Russia, Siberia and northern China; others, like the musk-deer and the goa, or Tibetan gazelle, are related to more northerly forms but have evolved into rather different species. A few, such as the coarse-coated Thorold's deer with its white lips and strange white antlers, have their closest relatives in the tropical forests of Burma; and there are a few that are quite unique with no close relatives anywhere else, like the blue sheep or Bharal, the chiru or Tibetan antelope, and the huge shaggy-coated wild ox, the yak.

Tibet has one member of the Equidae—the kiang or Tibetan wild ass. Like the goa and the wild yak, the kiang is found nowhere else but the Tibetan plateau. Indeed, these three animals more than any other are best suited to this environment for they are found, in given localities, all over the plateau, whereas many others are confined to certain portions of it—Thorold's deer, for example, is restricted to the eastern end of the plateau, in Szechwan. The plateau is bordered by the Himalayas in the south, by the Kuen-lun and Nan-shan ranges in the north, beyond which the plateau slopes gradually to the Gobi, and by the Pamir and Tian-shan in the west. At its eastern rim the rivers have cut massive gorges thousands of feet deep. These include the upper courses of the Yangtse, Yalung and Mekong, which rise in the north-east of the plateau and run south, cutting deeper and deeper as they go. Also in the north-east lies the source of the Hwang-Ho, which runs east and quickly leaves the plateau. East of the gorges, the plateau falls away to the Chinese plain, the slopes clothed in forest. The plateau itself is not flat but undulating and variable, broken by rocky parallel east–west running ridges. The Indus and Brahmaputra rivers rise to the north of the Himalayas—one running west, the other east—before turning south, cutting gorges through the mountains into the Indian peninsula. In the north-east is a region of broad lakes, the largest being Kukunor or Ching H'ai; and again in the south-west is the lakeland of Gnari-khorsum or Hundes, just east of where the plateau spills over the Indian border into Ladakh.

Ernst Schäfer, who explored much of the plateau in the 1930s, has divided it into three ecological zones. The gazelle-steppe, between 13,000 and 13,500ft, is the typical home of the goa. It merges on its south-eastern edge with the forest zone of Szechwan; and on the plateau it is found in sporadic isolated patches, since little of the plateau is even at this height. Alpine and sub-alpine grasses and vegetation, such as *Leontopodium*, predominate, with the vegetation season lasting for 4–5 months. It is here that the Tibetan nomads live; the swift gazelles can outrun men on horseback, and only the man with the high-powered rifle threatens them.

The kiang-steppe lies above this, and extends up to 15,750ft. Broad plains 15–20 miles across with flat, xerophyllous vegetation, are separated by bare eroded mountain ranges and swampy valleys. Here, the vegetation season lasts only 2–3 months. Gazelles range up to these heights in summer, and the wild yak comes down to this level in midwinter.

The highest zone is the wild-yak-steppe, a bitter windswept desert, almost sterile, with a growing season of 1–2 months only. Few human beings venture up to this altitude, which extends right up to the bare rock and permanent snows which begin at 19,000ft. The world's largest wild ox wanders in small herds over the barren plains, descending to the kiang-steppe in winter only.

Characteristics of the kiang

The kiang (*Equus kiang*) is the largest species of wild ass; those of the eastern plateau, in Szechwan, stand 142cm at the shoulder, the females weighing 250–300kg, and males often even 400kg. It has a large head, held high, with a thick muzzle and convex 'roman' nose; hard thick lips and a horny palate; a thick neck, especially in males, with a long upright mane; a short body and long robust limbs, broad hooves and a deep incisure between hooves and fetlocks; and a tail which is tufted at the tip and in

Page 89 (above) *Grant's zebra*. Equus burchelli boehmi, *in Lake Manyara National Park, Tanzania. The zebra on the right has well-marked shadow-stripes;* (below) *the dazzlingly marked Grévy's zebra*, Equus grevyi, *in the arid country of Kenya's northern frontier district*

The maneless zebra of Karamoja, north-eastern Uganda—a pair in Hanover zoo

addition has long hairs growing up either side. The summer coat is bright clear red; the winter coat is more brown, and very long and thick. There is a well-marked black dorsal stripe. The underparts are pure white, and this colour extends in wedges almost to the dorsal stripe, separating the coloured areas into shoulder, flank and haunch blocks. The white also extends on to the legs, where it is infused with the red of the body colour; on to the throat and sides of the neck, restricting the body-colour to a narrow strip on either side of the mane; and on to the muzzle, the insides of the ears, and as rings round the eyes.

Kiangs live in herds, which vary in size from 5–10 head up to 300 or 400. The herds wander over the wide moorlands, crossing the barren rocky ridges by low passes, which become well worn by constant use. Adult males of 7–8 years or more tend to stay apart from the herd, living alone for much of the year, combining in winter into small troops of up to 10. The stallions stay in higher, undulating country, coming down to the plains only when food has become scarce in the hills. The big herds consist of females with their young, younger males and females, and half-grown foals; each herd is led by an old mare. The herd is very cohesive, never becomes scattered, and moves strung out in file, following the leader and copying her every movement.

Kiangs feed on grass and low-growing plants, particularly the tough, sharp swamp grass, rich in silicic acid, which would cut and lacerate the more sensitive mouths of any other equid. On the kiang-steppe, there is only good feed in August and September; the kiangs put on fat at this time, becoming sleek and well-padded especially on the rump, flanks, neck and chest, and lining the inside of the body cavity with fat. As much as 40–45 kg may be put on in this way by big stallions. After September, the climate becomes steadily harsher, cold and dry; the streams freeze over, and kiang herds can be seen breaking the ice with their hooves. Then in January comes the snow, and although they continue to seek open streams or waterholes, they can eat the

F

snow and obtain their moisture from it. By May, afternoon snow-storms are still a regular feature; but the weather is improving and the young grass is beginning to sprout. In June 1935, the whole local kiang population came to graze in the upper Yalung valley of Szechwan, and in this limited region over 1,000 could be seen in a single day. In the warm weather, the herds often swim across the rivers and seem to take pleasure in bathing, which may assist them in moulting.

The stallions begin to follow the herds from about the end of July, but the mares drive them off with much shrill whinnying. By mid-August the males become restless and the air is full of their shrill nasal cries as they begin to herd the females, chasing them and rounding them up, and defending them against rival stallions. The males fight bitterly, rearing against each other and biting each other on the mane, neck and back, causing great scars. The rut ends in mid-September. The mares are pregnant all winter and the gestation lasts nearly a year, foals being born in late July or early August, so that a mare would expect to foal once every 2 years. The gravid mares collect in troops of 2–5, moving to rocky protected places where they drop their foals. The foals, as in all equids, can walk and run in a few hours, and follow their mothers from shortly after birth. They are leggy and have fleecy grey-brown coats. After a few weeks, mothers and foals rejoin the herd. Growth is rapid: already by the beginning of winter the foals are half-grown, and after the end of the first year they are independent of their mothers—often after forcible separation as a rutting stallion herds the mares, driving off the yearlings. But the only evidence we have of the age at sexual maturity indicates that this may be delayed—a captive male studied by Antonius had not shown any signs of sexual maturity at $3\frac{1}{2}$ years.

The kiang's coat is short and sleek in summer, but by August the new longer hair is beginning to show through, and it gets longer and thicker until midwinter. No underwool grows until the winter sets in. In spring, the winter coat is shed; the first traces of moult often appear at the end of April, while night temperatures are still falling as low as 10° C (50° F), although by day it may get as hot as 35° C (95° F). In early May the moult truly begins, first around the eyes and cheeks, followed 2–3 days later by shedding on the limbs, backs of the thighs, and base of the tail. A fortnight after the onset of moult, winter hair is shed from the throat and shoulders, and over the next 7 weeks the zones extend over the whole body, until after 10 weeks it remains only on the belly. Moulting is complete only after 80 days, near the end of July, so that full summer coat lasts for only a month. The coat is changing almost throughout the year: most actively at the beginning of the fertile season, and comes to a complete standstill only in the hardest winter months. The summer hairs are only 14–16mm long, but the long woolly winter coat hairs measure 35–45mm.

Kiang have keenly developed senses. In a good wind, they can scent a man between 400 and 500 yards, and they can see him nearly a mile away. Schäfer would approach them on horseback; if aware of his presence they would wait until he was about 400 yards away, then canter off, the herd strung out in typical fashion in a line behind the leader. After a short distance they stop and look back, even returning for a closer look before fleeing again. Foals, less wary and more curious than the rest, would approach him to within 150 or 200 yards. He describes how, when they were conscious of his presence but not sure of his whereabouts, all the heads would go up, nostrils flared, sniffing the wind, the whole herd pawing the ground and circling round like schooled horses, even rearing on their hind legs, their tails directed backwards.

Although the herd is so cohesive, its members running, wheeling and turning, sniffing, grazing, and drinking in unison, there is little actual physical contact between its members. There is little mutual grooming, unlike horses; a kiang will bite his own skin or scratch himself with his hoof, but the social skin-care sessions so conspicuous in a herd of Przewalski horses rarely, if ever, occur. Captive kiangs are usually rather restless, even aggressive, at least when in an open paddock; but indoors in the stable they quieten down and permit themselves to be scratched for a short time.

The name kiang seems to be an attempt at their Tibetan name, *Djang*. To the Tibetans they are sacred animals, not to be killed, and they are greatly shocked when Europeans or Chinese desire to hunt them. Although Schäfer was collecting specimens for scientific purposes, he did not relish doing so, and was impressed by the beauty and splendour of the wild herds. Apart from man, the kiang's only enemy is said to be the wolf; packs of wolves follow the herd and separate out a young or sick animal which they then run down and overpower.

The kiang has not been domesticated, although some local horses, such as the Ablac breed of Bhutan, somewhat resemble kiangs in colour and have been thought in the past to be derived from them. Tibetans claim that kiang stallions come into their camps at night and mingle with the tanghans (the hardy little Tibetan ponies), covering the mares who later give birth to hybrids. These supposed hybrids are called 'Si-ming horses', as they are said to be bred deliberately by the nomads of Si-ming in Kansu; but one of these animals, examined by Schäfer, turned out to be an ordinary pony of slightly unusual coloration. It is very doubtful whether hybridisation does in fact occur under such conditions, although it has been successfully undertaken in captivity.

Distribution of the kiang

Kiangs are sporadically, but not continuously, distributed over the Tibetan plateau. They occur in the Altyn Tagh range on the northern flank of the tableland, east as far as Kukunor and south to Seshu-Gomba on the Yalung river. In the eastern region their range is broken up by the massive gorges; to the south-west they are found, wherever there is kiang-steppe, as far as the Chumbi valley, south of Lhasa. From this latter region they are said sometimes to wander through the Himalayan passes into Sikkhim. These southern kiangs, south of the upper Brahmaputra, are much smaller than the big north-eastern ones, only 100–15cm high. Then there is a break, and kiangs do not occur again until we reach the south-western edge of the plateau, at Gnarikhorsum and over the Indian border into Ladakh and the 'Little Tibet' region. The western kiangs are slightly, though not markedly, smaller than the Kukunor ones, differing mainly in their much darker colour—a beautiful deep auburn in winter—and the greater downward extension of the darker areas on the flanks.

Wild asses are found not only in Tibet, but in other desert areas of Asia too, and in the deserts of north-eastern Africa. Everyone

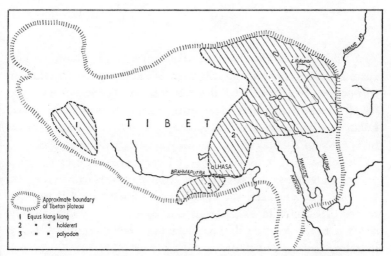

Fig 5 *Approximate distribution of* Equus kiang, *the kiang*

agrees that the African wild ass is a distinct species, *Equus africanus*, but there has been some controversy over whether or not the kiang and the other Asiatic wild asses are separate species, or just races of a single species. Modern classifications, however, keep them apart, and it does seem as if in appearance, behaviour, climatic tolerance and so on they are certainly as distinct as either of them is from the African wild ass. All asses differ from horses in that they have rather longer ears, are shorter, have thinner manes, lack long hairs on the tail, and have chestnuts on the forelimbs only. Their skulls are shorter and broader with a longer bony ear tube, they have a square occipital crest, a greater angle between face and braincase, a shorter palate and a narrower muzzle. The enamel patterns of the teeth are less complex, and the so-called 'wolf-tooth'—the small, peg-like first premolar—is usually retained into adult life which it never is in the horse. The underparts are light-coloured, as they often are in the horse, as are the legs, which in horses are usually dark.

ONAGERS

The wild asses of the Asiatic lowland deserts all belong to one species, *Equus hemionus*, but there are six geographic varieties, or subspecies, which will be described later. These varieties are usually known by their local names—dzigguetai in Mongolia, kulan in Turkestan, khur in Kutch, ghor-khan in Iran, achdari in Syria—but the species as a whole can be called the onager.

The name onager comes from the Greek, ὀνάγρος literally 'wild ass', contracted and latinised by the Romans as onagrus or onager. By some quirk of fate, the Greeks and Romans used it to refer to the African wild ass, but in our day it has become firmly attached to the Asiatic wild ass, which the Greeks knew as ἡμίωνος literally, 'half-ass', or mule.

Onagers, wherever they are found, differ from kiangs in these respects: they are smaller, have smaller heads, narrower snouts, longer ears, shorter manes, a lack of long hairs on the sides of the tail (except in some newborn foals), smaller chestnuts, more slender limbs with longer distal segments, broader, more rounded rumps, and the details of the skull and teeth vary. Also their colour is lighter in winter and less red in summer; the wedge of white behind the shoulder is narrower, leaving the darker flank-patch more squared off in shape; their buttocks are white, not infused with red; and there is less white on the neck. Finally, the sequence of events in the spring moult is different, for not only does the moult take a shorter time, but it begins on the face and belly, then on the knees and hocks or the limbs, quickly spreading over the whole body, falling last from the back, elbow and angle of the jaw.

The distribution of the onager is uneven, not like the kiang, because of the absence of a suitable habitat, but because of human interference. In the time of Homer they were found in Anatolia; in the mid-eighteenth century, there were still herds living on the steppes west of the Urals. Even at the beginning of the present century the range, although it had shrunk somewhat at the edges, was still virtually continuous from the Gobi desert and Lake Baikal, west into Kazakhstan, and south through Turkmenia and Iran into the Thar desert of northern India, and the deserts of Palestine and northern Arabia. But everywhere onagers have been shot for sport and for food, and for their skins which are made into mats; most of all, the land they live on is needed for human habitation, irrigated agriculture and so on. So the range has shrunk still further and has broken up into four small, discontinuous segments.

The largest of these segments is in Mongolia. Here, reputedly, onagers are still fairly numerous; both in the Gobi itself and on its western edges, and the distribution spills over the border into Dzungaria, in the Chinese province of Sinkiang. Possibly a few still stray from time to time through the Dzungarian Gates, between the Tienshan and Altai ranges, into Soviet territory. No one knows how many there are in this area: probably several thousand. But they are not protected, and now that the Mongolian People's Republic has opened its doors to American hunting parties, the situation will have to be watched very carefully.

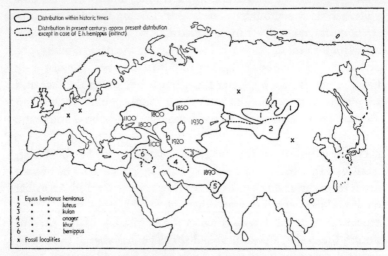

Fig 6   *Distribution of the onager,* Equus hemionus, *within historical times and during the present century*

Another unprotected, and much smaller population, roams the deserts of Dasht-i-Lut and Dasht-i-Kevir in Iran. These are the pathetic remnants of the huge herds that once migrated back and forth across the great Persian deserts up into the high desert valleys in summer, and down into the low lying areas in winter. In the last century there was a big herd that lived in winter on the high plain, 5,500–7,000ft up, between Dehbid and Isfahan; and as late as 1910, the Swedish explorer Sven Hedin found them only a little east of Teheran. They are protected only on paper, and apparently still hunted on occasion. They survive only because their remaining habitat is too sterile for human occupation, but it is surely only a matter of time before Iran's exploding population dislodges them from here too. In the meantime, however, a holding action has had some success. There were only 300 ten years ago, and now there are over a thousand.

There is another small population living in the Little Rann of Kutch, just on the Indian side of the border with Pakistan. This is precisely the area where the border is least defined, and there has already been one minor war in the area, when the tanks rolled across the great salt desert, and Hindu and Moslem slaughtered each other for the sake of national pride. And the onagers suffered too. In 1962 there had been 870 in the Little Rann; an aerial count made at the end of 1969 showed just 368.

The position of the fourth population is far more satisfactory. Although they are quite gone from the Kyzyl Kum and Kara Kum and the steppes of Kazakhstan, there is still a small population, numbering some 800, in the Badkhyz Reserve in southern Turkmenia, on the Afghan border. A few may live in Afghanistan too, and some migrate annually between Afghanistan and the reserve; but in Badkhyz at least they are well protected, and have been the object of intensive ecological research—much still unpublished—by Soviet scientists, especially A. O. Solomatin and V. G. Heptner. From Badkhyz a small number have been naturalised on Barsa Kelmes, an island in the Aral Sea.

The races of the onager

The two largest subspecies are those found in Mongolia. Both the North Mongolian and the Gobi dziggetai stand from 117–42cm at the shoulder. The former has, like the kiang, what is known as a 'disruptive' coloration, with reddish patches on head, neck, shoulders, flanks and haunches, sharply marked off from the white underside; and the dorsal stripe is broad (55–70mm wide), with a well-marked white border on either side especially in the young which becomes obliterated with age. The

Gobi race has, on the contrary, an 'intergrading' form of colour pattern: the darker patches are pale buff and the undersides are light yellowish, the two colours grading into each other. The dorsal stripe is much narrower in the Gobi race, and there is never at any age a light border. There are also skull differences between the two subspecies. Most of those surviving today are undoubtedly of the Gobi race, although the well-known Russian zoologist Professor Bannikov photographed a living specimen of the North Mongolian form near the Mongolia–Dzungaria border in 1959. How widely the Gobi subspecies was distributed in the past is uncertain, although it is known to have occurred not only in Mongolia but into the Chinese provinces of Sinkiang (at Kichik-Ulan-Ussu) and Kansu (at Surin-Gol); and it may indeed still exist over most of its former range. This is not likely for the North Mongolian subspecies, however: its range formerly extended from Dauriya and Transbaikalia in the east, along the comparatively fertile strip south of the Altai mountains in northern Mongolia, through the Dzungarian Gates and into Soviet territory as far as Zaisan Nor and perhaps the Semipalatinsk region. Quite certainly it is gone today from the eastern half of this range, and very likely from Zaisan Nor as well.

The kulan or Turkmenian wild ass and the ghor-khar or Persian wild ass are smaller than the Mongolian forms—standing 110–27cm, and averaging 117–20cm at the shoulder—and in some respects resemble each other, for they both have a disruptive colour pattern like the North Mongolian race but less striking, and a broad dorsal stripe (60–80mm broad in summer coat, 70–90mm in winter) bordered with white on either side. However, the kulan has more colour gradation in its summer coat than the ghor-khar, with sandy-yellow or pale buff upper parts grading into white below; while the reddish buff of the ghor-khar is rather more sharply marked from the white though the white itself is less 'clean'. In winter, the kulan has a very thick yellow-brown coat, while that of the ghor-khar is darker, less thick but more curled. In the kulan, the white does not extend as high up the flanks, but cuts across the jaw angle instead of following the line of it. The main difference between the two, however, is in the shape of the skull, which is broader in the kulan with a longer snout and longer occiput.

The khur or Indian wild ass stands about the same height as the Persian and Turkmenian forms, but differs from them in both colour and skull shape. The colour in summer coat is darker—grey-fawn to reddish yellow-grey—but the white of the under-parts extends higher up the flanks, to about the halfway line or more. In winter, the colour is greyish to pale chestnut; the winter coat is short, and does not differ appreciably from the summer coat in length. Unlike other races, the dorsal stripe does not extend down the tail, but fades away halfway down; and there is no dark ring round the hooves such as occurs in adults of all other subspecies. In the skull, the nasal bones are raised, forming a bump on the snout of the living animal and evidently increasing the size of the nasal cavity, moistening the dry desert air before it is breathed into the lungs.

The range of the khur was probably always restricted to the Thar desert in the north-west of the Indian peninsula. The ghor-khar on the other hand existed all over the Iranian plateau, extending some distance into Pakistan; a specimen intermediate between the two races was collected in the 1880s on the Sham Plains, Baluchistan, at the foot of the Iranian plateau.

The smallest, and perhaps most distinctive, of the onagers no longer exists at all. This was the achdari or Syrian wild ass; only 1m in height, a bright tawny-olive colour in summer, grading into the buff colour of the underside, with a short, light reddish-coloured winter coat. The skull was like a very small version of the khur's with the same raised nasal bones. This was the wild ass of the Bible, the onager of the Vulgate. Its range formerly extended from Palestine, northern Arabia, even perhaps southern Turkey, east across Mesopotamia to the Zagros mountains in

Iran, which separated its distribution from that of the Persian subspecies. As late as 1850, Layard, the discoverer of Nineveh, reported that wild asses were caught as foals by Arabs in the Sinjar region west of Mosul; in 1862, Rawlinson wrote of the herds he had seen while digging in Assyria. But by the turn of the century they were already scarce; the last one known to exist died in the Schonnbrunn zoo, Vienna, in 1927. The American ecologist, Lee Talbot, searching for them in 1960, failed to find any; the Bedouin told him, 'our fathers knew them'.

The habitat of the onager

The environment in which the onager lives is in its way as harsh as that of the kiang, but there is no altitude problem, and the hot summer season is longer; but the ground is even less fertile, and for much of the year there is almost no surface water. In the Iranian desert, summer temperatures are claimed to rise to 58° C (136° F) in the heat of the day, falling to 15° C (59° F) at night. Arnulf Johannes, catching onagers in Iran for Hagenbeck, was awed by the burning heat and barrenness of terrain where he found them in July: no shade, no trees, not another living thing—no bird, no insect, not even a scorpion—nothing but the flat desert and the shimmering mirages.

In the Badkhyz Reserve, the onagers move to the watering-places in early May and stay by them, not moving more than 10 miles or so from them so long as they still exist. But for most of the year they feed on the juicy low-growing succulents which absorb moisture from the atmosphere, particularly at night. The commonest items in the diet are the succulent *Carex*, and three species of grass; but the diet changes from one season to another according to the nutritive content of the food-plants, and 110 species of food-plants have so far been identified. They also eat the salty soil of their habitat, and blocks of salt have to be supplied in captivity for them to lick. During the cold weather the pastures contract and the kulan may have to scrape through the snow with their hooves to find food. At this time, the asses come together into large herds; in Badkhyz as many as 300 kulans come together at certain times of the year, particularly in winter and summer, splitting up again in spring and autumn.

Social organisation of onagers

As with the kiang, onager herds are led by an old female and consist mainly of females and young males, the males living apart for most of the year; some males, however, do appear to live in the big kulan herds, and Solomatin states that one of them takes some of the leadership roles. The herds often run together with herds of goitred gazelle, which live in the same dry country. The rut takes place in early summer, not in late summer as with kiangs; gestation is said to average 11 months (335 days) in the khur, 12 months (368 days) in the ghor-khar and kulan; but in the kulan both the rut and births take place in late April and early May, whereas they are later—June or early July—in the ghor-khar. There is, therefore, a 2 year space between births for each mare. When due to give birth, mares leave the herd singly or in small groups to drop their foals, and return to it 3 months later. Lactation lasts for $1-1\frac{1}{2}$ years; the young do not grow as fast as do young kiangs, and they are not sexually mature for 2 years; the females do not therefore foal until they are 3 years old. In the stallion, sexual maturity is later than in the mare; the testes do not descend until he is 26 months old.

At birth, the sex ratio is very nearly equal, 1·1 males : 1 female; during the first year, female mortality is greater, and among yearlings the ratio is 1·6 : 1; but subsequently the trend is reversed and the adult sex ratio was given by Solomatin as 4·5 females : 1 male in 1959. The birth-rate in that year and several preceding years was 19 per cent, and the death-rate 10 per cent, so that the population was in fact increasing by 9 per cent per annum: under normal conditions, of course, the birth- and death-rates would be equal, and we must unfortunately assume that in the Kutch onager population the death-rate exceeds the birth-rate because of their decreasing numbers.

Moulting

The spring moult in the onager begins in March or early April —somewhat earlier in older animals, later in youngsters. The length of time taken over the moult varies with the length and thickness of the winter coat, and the severity of the climate: in Iran it is said to take only 2–3 weeks, and in captivity in Europe it usually finished by June; in Badkhyz it ends in mid-June; in Mongolia the male's moult finishes by the end of June, but the female's continues until mid-July. Hairs of the summer coat in all three areas are about 18–24cm long, but the winter coats differ: in kulans the winter hair is twice this length, in Iran less, in Mongolia more. It has already been described how the sequence of shedding differs from the kiang; but in all races of onagers so far studied it is much the same, falling first from the belly rather than from the legs as in the kiang, though a small strip may remain on the belly till the end. The summer coat lasts until early October, when winter hair begins to appear on the dorsum: the winter coat takes 6–8 weeks to grow in.

It should not be thought that the timing and duration of the moult is entirely unvarying or genetically determined, although certainly the sequence is: but in cold years it is somewhat delayed, and it was found that a captive group from Iran in their first winter in Hamburg zoo grew longer winter coats than in subsequent winters.

Young onagers are born with long fleecy coats; these are shed early in life—after 2–3 weeks in Iranian onagers but only after nearly 8 weeks in Turkmenian, the process taking altogether about 40 days.

Like all equids, onagers keep their skin in good condition by biting, scratching and rolling, although unlike horses they do not bite the moulting patches to loosen them. Like horses, and unlike kiangs, mutual grooming is common, two animals standing counter-parallel, nipping each others' flanks and necks, for long periods of time.

Stamina and temperament of onagers

The onager is a swift and tireless courser; in Solomatin's opinion it is built even better, in some respects, than a riding horse. A herd of Indian wild asses was timed by the famous Anglo-Indian naturalist, the late E. P. Gee, at an average of 28mph for nearly half an hour, reaching over 30mph for short bursts, until the asses reached an area of particularly rough ground where the motor vehicle could not follow. Erna Mohr records that during a capture expedition a female Persian onager was chased for over three-quarters of an hour at nearly 30mph; at the end of the chase the animal was caught, but was still not sweating! During this same expedition, two onagers jumped a wall 7½ft high. In the wild, especially in Badkhyz, they are known to climb very steep inclines in their regular migration routes, and hard excrescences on the outer sides of the hoofs probably help in finding a foothold.

Onagers are wild and restless in captivity, more so even than zebras; they do, however, come to recognise their keepers and a few other people, and allow these people to scratch them, even presenting their necks or crupper to be scratched. Fortunately they breed well in captivity. Most of the Persian stock are descended from 24 animals (12 of each sex) captured by the 1954 Hagenbeck expedition to Iran, which have now bred well into the fourth generation and have become self-perpetuating. A studbook of them was started by the late Erna Mohr and is now kept by Hamburg zoo, where the largest herd still lives. There is a good stock of kulans, derived from Badkhyz, in several zoos; and a few khurs are kept in Indian zoos.

AFRICAN WILD ASSES

The third and last species of wild ass is the African wild ass (*Equus africanus*). Leaner than the Asiatic species and with the long ears of the domestic donkey, this species is the most extreme of the three: if the kiang is the most horselike, the African wild ass is the least, with the onager intermediate. Like the horse, the kiang has broad hooves, the onager has narrower ones, and the African wild ass has narrow, vertical hooves suitable for rocky desert areas. The tail is tufted, even in foals, and the chestnuts are very small. The colour in the African species is usually some shade of grey, grading insensibly into the white underparts; the legs and muzzle are white as in Asiatic wild asses, and there are traces of the same white wedges separating shoulder, flank and haunch blocks of colour. The mane is thin and rather sparse but long and upright like the kiang's or indeed like a wild horse's. The dorsal stripe is thin and black, and may disappear and reappear, and there is always either a black transverse stripe across the shoulders or zebra stripes on the legs, or both—these being the full expression of markings which often occur as traces in other wild asses, even in horses. There are also distinctive features in the skull and teeth.

It has often been stated that Asiatic wild asses are distinguishable from African ones, as well as from horses, by their long, slender metapodials (the cannon and shannon bones forming the lower segments of the limbs). The situation is actually more complicated than that. The longest metapodials, relative to the length of the upper limb segments (up to 80 per cent of the upper segment length) are found in the kiang and in the domestic donkey, followed by most subspecies of onager; the Indian

Page 107   (above) *Somali wild asses in the low-lying Danakil plain, northern Ethiopia;* (below) *Persian onagers,* Equus hemionus onager, *in May during the moult. At this time mutual skin care rituals are very important*

Page 108 (above) *A kulan foal takes its first steps at Badkhys Reserve, Turkmenistan;* (below) *a half-grown kulan foal, showing the shoulder-stripe which is quite often seen in Persian and Turkmenian wild asses*

onager (khur) alone among onagers has rather shorter meta-podials, with African wild asses and horses having the shortest of all, only 65–70 per cent of the length of the upper segments of the limbs (radius and tibia). Slenderness of metapodials follows a different scheme. Here the onagers (except the khur, again) have clearly the most slender metapodials, the breadth at their upper ends being less than 20 per cent of the length; followed by the kiang, with domestic donkeys, African wild asses, the khur, and horses having the broadest (up to 25 per cent).

Races of African wild ass

The living African wild asses fall into two clearly defined sub-species: the Nubian wild ass, which stands 110–22cm at the shoulder (although specimens of 140cm have been claimed) and has no leg-stripes but always has a well-marked shoulder-cross; and the Somali wild ass, which is larger, about 127cm high, and has well-marked leg-stripes but usually no shoulder-cross. The Nubian race is grey with a strong reddish tinge in summer, the Somali having more of a buff or yellow cast. Both are greyer in winter—indeed, the winter coat is hardly longer than the summer coat since there is little seasonality in the environment.

There are also differences in the skull and teeth; the Somali race has a longer diastema and higher face, and there is a curious enamel fold, the 'metaconid-metastylid bridge', on some of the cheekteeth.

There is considerable variability in the skin markings of both subspecies. In the Nubian subspecies, two types of shoulder-stripe may occur, neither of which resembles the long, bold stripe of domestic donkeys. One type is very short, scarcely visible in side-view but boldly marked; the other is long, thin, and rather faint. I have seen only 9 pure-bred specimens—7 preserved skins, and 2 living animals (not including the offspring of the two, also one aberrant individual) and of these 5 have the short type and 4 the long thin type. In the Somali race, the shoulder-cross is usually not developed, but out of 13 pure-bred specimens, I have seen 4 which do have one (of the long thin type), as well as one which has a stripe on one side only.

In the Somali wild ass also the dorsal stripe is very often incomplete, fading out on the lumbar region and reappearing on the crupper: it is always complete in the Nubian. The leg-stripes always exist in the Somali, but never in the Nubian are there more than faint brownish marks on the fetlocks. Occasional odd specimens may have a bifurcated shoulder-stripe, or weak traces of body-stripes; while one extraordinary specimen in the Vienna zoo has no stripes at all but a peculiar dappled pattern all over the body.

Habitat and distribution of African wild asses

Both races live in flat, arid, stony regions dotted with hillocks which are used as observation posts. The temperature may soar up to 50° C (122° F) in the daytime; this is probably the most inhospitable of any region occupied by wild asses. Here the wild asses live in small troops of up to 10, the older males separately, and the bisexual herds are led by an old female. They graze from early dawn up to 10am, lying up in the heat of the day under the sparse vegetation, and feed again from about 5pm until sundown. Water is a considerable problem and the wild asses are capable of going without drinking for 2–3 days; they may travel long distances at night to visit waterholes.

When chased, Somali wild asses begin running when the pursuer is still a long way off; they do not run continuously, but every so often stop and look back. A wild ass of this race has been clocked in a car at 30mph. When caught, they defend themselves by kicking and biting.

The distribution of the Somali wild ass is centred on northern

Somalia, especially the former British section. From here they used to be found well into Eritrea, probably along the coast to where the Ethiopian highlands come down to the sea at Zulla; and south into Ogaden, from where there was a seasonal migration to the Nogal valley across the Somali border. They were seen near Imi, Ogaden, in the 1940s, and in 1970 four were captured for Basel zoo in the Nogal valley. A few hundred still exist in the great Salt Plain, 400ft below sea-level in the Danakil depression, where they are protected by the Ethiopian government; here their existence is not threatened, as the habitat is unsuitable for domestic stock. In the old days they were under the strict protection of the Sultan of Aussa, and any man who killed a wild ass, would have his hand cut off.

From time to time, unusually small and rather dark wild asses with the usual leg-stripes but with a strikingly long, bold shoulder-stripe turn up in herds of the Somali race especially in Eritrea. It was thought for a long time that these represented a different race, even a different species, and the name *Equus* or *Asinus taeniopus* was given to them. It has become clear, however, that they are in fact hybrids between Somali wild asses and domestic donkeys. The Italian naturalist Major Ziccardi has described how the local people, especially the Danakil of Eritrea, often leave she-donkeys beside waterholes overnight, hoping that wild stallions will cover them: in this way, they hope to improve the breed, and the frequency with which Danakil donkeys bear traces of leg-stripes testifies to the efficiency of this. However, it often works the other way, and the donkey runs off with the wild asses, and her hybrid offspring is born wild. The hybrids seem to survive in the wild better than their mothers, but they in turn are less viable than the pure-bred wild asses and seem rarely, if ever, to reproduce themselves. A pair of wild asses of this description was photographed by the Italian Pellegrini at Wadi Dudo in 1957, and in 1969 a captured one was shown to Jeffrey Boswall of the BBC as a wild ass.

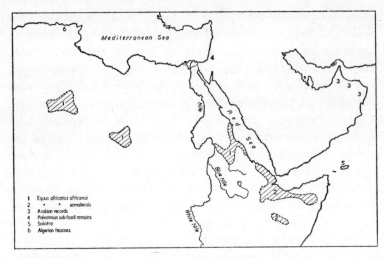

Fig 7   *Recent distribution of* Equus africanus, *including subfossil and possible feral populations*

It seems likely that the Nubian wild ass once ranged from the Red Sea coast west across the Nile to the Sahara massifs of Tibesti and Hoggar; and from northern Eritrea, thence north of the Gulf of Zulla into Upper Egypt. All authorities agree that it occurred in the Sudan deserts and jebels east of the Nile, but there has been some controversy over the central Saharan wild asses—whether they are not perhaps feral (that is, escaped from domestication) rather than truly wild. Some certainly are: the small dark asses photographed in the 1950s by Pellegrini were said to be owned by local people who sometimes rounded them up, and the low prestige that donkeys carry compared to other domestic stock such as camels, among the Sahara tribes like the Tuareg and Tibu, means that the escape rate will be very high. But there are, or were, truly wild asses there too, closely resembling the Nubian subspecies. Canon Tristram in 1860 gave a careful description of one including the statement that it stood 'two hands higher than the common (ie domestic) ass', as does the Nubian; and as recently as 1963 the anthropologist Nicolaisen published a photograph of a young wild ass, captured by Tuareg, with the thin shoulder-stripe seen commonly in Nubian wild asses.

But asses, whether feral or truly wild, are no longer common in the North African deserts. The wild ass is totally protected in the Sudan: but what exactly is it that is being protected? A few feral asses there certainly are, but records of undoubted Nubian wild asses are very few and far between, even since World War II. In 1935, Major Powell-Cotton and his daughter Diana shot a pair at Wadi Hafta, near Tokar in the Red Sea Hills; in the following year, Michael Mason saw a few troops and shot an aged female at Wadi Sharag in the same district. They were not recorded again until the naturalist Hans Schomber heard from an 'authoritative source' that there were some, at least in 1959, on the plains south of Erkowit. Since then, again nothing. It looks as if Nicolaisen's 1963 photograph from Hoggar may be the most recent record of this race.

If the Nubian wild ass is truly gone, then we are deprived of a creature of splendour and beauty. Those who have seen it in the wild declare that familiarity with the docile, lovable domestic donkey leaves one totally unprepared for the speed and sleekness and proud majesty of the wild ass. Perhaps because the donkey, meekly bowed under heavy loads, is such a familiar sight, the unrestrained freedom of his wild cousin is the more marvellous: he goes where he will, he runs with the wind and the sandstorm, he belongs to no one but the desert, he is liberty itself.

Michael Mason, in the Sudan, when he was asked by some English ladies at a garden-party if he wished to shoot a wild ass, snapped 'I would rather shoot a woman'. Hard-bitten big-game hunter that he was, he had been touched by the magic of the wild ass. When at last he found an aged mare, her limbs trembling, standing alone waiting for death, he did shoot her, as he put it, to save that noble old lady from the beastly mangling hyaenas, who would not wait for her to die.

It has long been known that some former inhabitants of North Africa—or perhaps they were the ancestors of the peoples who live there today—painted and engraved remarkable representations of their local fauna on the rock-faces of their homes. When the works were executed is not known—anything from 1,000–10,000 years ago. Surprisingly, they depict giraffes, elephants and elands: animals now only found hundreds of miles to the south, in more fertile scrub and grasslands; so it seems that in those days the Sahara was not as desolate as now. A wild ass appears among these animals in a fresco at Enfouss, northern Algeria, although it would not necessarily have lived in either the same time or the same place as the non-desert animals. Unexpectedly, the ass of the frescoes has leg-stripes and a long, strongly marked shoulder-cross. An ass of the same type is seen also on a Roman mosaic at Bone, Algeria. A subspecies, *Equus asinus atlanticus*, was described by Werth in 1930 on the evidence of the Enfouss fresco; this name had previously been given (1884) to a fossil jawbone from late Pleistocene deposits at Oued Seguen, Algeria, remarkable for its small size, but this jawbone has been found to belong to a zebra, so the name *atlanticus* cannot stand. In fact, there are no undisputed Pleistocene ass remains in Africa at all; it seems that wild asses are very recent immigrants into Africa, coming perhaps from south-west Asia. There was, however, by Roman times, a subspecies of wild ass with leg-stripes and a long, strong cross-stripe, in northern Algeria; and remains of Nubian wild asses are known from Neolithic sites in Egypt and the Sudan.

THE ORIGIN OF THE DONKEY

It seems reasonably well established that the species *Equus africanus* was broadly ancestral to domestic donkeys. The problem arises when trying to discover which subspecies was the ancestor, and therefore where donkeys were first domesticated.

The Nubian wild ass, usually invoked in this regard, makes an unsatisfactory ancestor for a number of reasons, as will be explained in Chapter 5; some donkeys, especially in Morocco and other parts of the eastern Mediterranean, have striped legs and so may be derived at least in part from the Algerian race. But for the ordinary grey donkey, with white unstriped legs, a strong shoulder-cross, cinnamon-coloured ears, and darker coloured narrower hooves than any known wild ass, there is as yet no plausible ancestor. So—where did it come from? Or, to put the question less directly, is there anywhere else in that general part of the world where wild asses might have lived?

Wild asses live in arid areas: broadly speaking, in deserts, though not of course in sand dunes but rather on stony plains, salt flats and bare, rocky hills. The lowland deserts of the Old World are found in North Africa (the Sahara), Somalia and neighbouring parts of Ethiopia (Eritrea, Ogaden), Arabia, the Middle East, northern India/Pakistan (the Thar), Turkestan, and Mongolia (the Gobi). In North Africa and Somalia we have Nubian, Somali and old-Algerian wild asses; in the Middle East, the achdari and ghor-khar; in the Thar, the khur; in Turkestan, the kulan; in Mongolia, the dziggetai. In Arabia . . . ?

On the island of Sokotra, south of Aden, there are wild asses. Though only some 80–100cm high, they are said to differ considerably from the domestic asses of that island. Henry Forbes, who drew attention to them in 1900, was struck by their bright coloration. They are, however, basically similar to donkeys, with a dark grey upperside, white underside, legs, muzzle and eye-ring, have long ears with cinnamon-coloured backs, and a long thick cross-stripe; and, as can be seen from two specimens in the British Museum, their skulls are just like those of donkeys.

Wilfred Thesiger, who explored the Empty Quarter in the 1940s, found wild asses in several places—in the hills round 'Ibri, in Wahiba country, around 'Ain Na'ama—and gave it as his opinion that they are indigenous, not feral. Later he shot two wild asses at Buraimi oasis: these, however, he did consider to be feral. (Their skins and skulls are in the British Museum: they do not differ from those of the Sokotra asses.) In the 1930s, H. St John Philby had also mentioned wild asses in the Empty Quarter, and in 1930 another explorer, the remarkable Raswan, also spoke of wild asses in Arabia.

So we know that there were free-living asses in Arabia, and probably still are: certainly, they exist on Sokotra. But, in spite of Thesiger's opinion, there is no proof that they are indigenous. The Sokotra asses are generally considered to have been left there by the frankincense-traders of ancient Egypt: again, there is no evidence either way, although in this case, since there are no other indigenous mammals, it is very probable that the asses were introduced from elsewhere.

The world, of course, is reasonably well-explored; if truly wild asses existed in Arabia, would they not have been discovered long since? One might think so; but for David Harrison, engaged in compiling his recent three-volume work, *Mammals of Arabia*, there were a lot of surprises in store—most of them from the Empty Quarter. As he was preparing volume 2, including descriptions of the Artiodactyla, a wild goat (*Capra aegagrus*) was captured in the Oman mountains and sent on his behalf to the London zoo. No wild goats were previously known from Arabia! No sooner was volume 2 completed and sent to press, in 1967, than he received a crate containing the mortal remains of a wild sheep, *Ovis ammon*, also from Oman, and another species new to Arabia.

Farther north, from both northern Arabia and Palestine, there had long been reports of two species of wild ass, co-existing in the desert wastes. The late Francis Harper, who collected abundant data on rare mammals, considered them mistaken—both types in fact being referable to the achdari. It is none the less intriguing that such reports should have come from just there, for when the ranges of two distinct but closely related species meet, they often overlap to some extent, there being an area where the two compete although they are exclusive occupants of most of their ranges.

As if to draw all these threads together, the archaeologist Ducos described the animal remains from a Neolithic site in Palestine, including mostly wild forms but some probably domestic. Among these are the remains of an ass, which he considered to be most likely wild. It is definitely not an onager, but possesses both the tooth characters and the relatively short, broad metapodials of *Equus africanus*—to an excessive degree in fact! The remains are those of a very big animal, as large as the largest *somaliensis*. Even if it was a domestic animal, we have here indisputable evidence for the very early occurrence of *Equus africanus* or its tame descendant, not only on Asiatic soil, but in the very region where this species had been claimed to exist in the wild state. Ducos gave it the name *Asinus palestinae*, but there is no evidence that it was specifically distinct from the African wild ass—it should therefore probably be called *Equus africanus palestinae*. There is no information what its skull was like, and of course nothing about its skin, so we are still no nearer to finding an ancestor for the domestic donkey—except that we seem to have strong circumstantial evidence for an extension of the range of *Equus africanus* outside Africa.

FERAL ASSES

Like horses, donkeys have a tendency to escape from confinement and run wild: in other words, to become feral. Whether or not there are pure wild asses in the Sahara or in Arabia, there are certainly plenty of feral ones there. The donkeys of Sokotra have already been mentioned. There are feral donkeys in the arid country of northern Kenya, in eastern Ethiopia, and in the Ethiopia-Sudan borderlands. Europe has its feral donkeys, too; there are some in southern Spain, and a well-established population of about 100 on Tavolara Island, off the northern coast of Sardinia.

In Australia and in North America there are feral asses just as there are feral horses: living in more arid, stony country than the wild horses, they keep out of man's way more successfully but they, too, are unpopular and much persecuted. In Australia, the donkeys that ran wild are descended from a number that were introduced for farms and mines in the late nineteenth century: they carried supplies from Carnarvon to the Kimberleys, and from the Victoria River Depot, near Timber Creek, to Victoria River Downs. In 1956 it is estimated that there were about 150,000 living wild in the Victoria River District, and they have spread far and wide from this centre. Since 1961 there have been bounties on them since it is said that they contribute to erosion by eating out river frontages; and they are full of parasites which can infect domestic animals. Thousands of them are shot each year, but still they thrive.

In the desert lands of North America, feral asses—known as burros—are common from Mexico to central Idaho; some are escapees, mostly from pack animals in Spanish settlements, some were deliberately turned loose on to the range. In California, where there are about 5,000, they live in the hills round Death Valley, Panamint Valley and Saline Valley in Inyo County, and between highways 91 and 66 in central and eastern San Bernardino County; the other major concentration, slightly larger, is along the Colorado river from Utah to the Mexican border, with most being in Arizona. They favour steep-walled canyons and stony ground, but avoid both flat lands and extreme rough country. Their ranges centre around waterholes, and in summer when it is dry they never wander more than 5 or 6 miles from a waterhole, but they are also capable of digging in dry stream beds, 4–5ft down until they hit water. In winter they tend to move to lower ground but there are no regular migration routes; on the whole, they drop their foals in spring, but there is no marked seasonality in breeding. During the rut, the jack gathers his harem of jennies and defends them bitterly against other jacks.

The burro is a remarkable animal in many ways, not least because he is more adaptable even than the indigenous wild sheep, the bighorn. There is a fear, indeed, that he is out-competing the bighorn in many ranges: his diet is more flexible (he even eats creosote bushes!), he is less susceptible to disease and he has large, noisy troops which scare bighorn away. In addition, he tramples vegetation and pollutes waterholes. Like mustangs, burros are shot, poisoned and rounded up in large numbers; but again like mustangs, there is a growing feeling that a place ought to be found for them.

FOSSIL WILD ASSES

During the upper Pleistocene, asses were found way outside their present ranges and had penetrated into Europe. During Mousterian times—when the last Ice Age had swept over Europe, and Neanderthal man lived and hunted in western Europe, between 70,000 and 30,000 years ago—a species of ass known as *Equus hydruntinus* was common on the tundra and loess steppe south of the great ice-sheets. The skull of this ass is unknown, but its metapodials were long and slender like an onager's, and the low-crowned teeth, like *Equus africanus*, were different from any living species, and more primitive. The Mousterian *Equus hydruntinus* was about the size of a kulan or ghor-khar, but the species had entered Europe (we do not know where from: perhaps indeed it had evolved there) earlier, in the previous interglacial, as a larger animal, kiang-sized—so had become smaller in the course of time. The remains of the species occur mostly in northern Europe; it was replaced in Italy by a different species, *Equus graziosii*, so far poorly known but again with slender limbs, and rather smaller in size.

At the end of the Mousterian phase there was a temporary recession of the ice, opening up ice-free routes into Europe from the outside world. Neanderthal man disappeared with an extraordinary rapidity and was replaced by men of completely modern type who remained even after the ice-sheets' return: maybe the Neanderthal physique was no longer adaptive, and there was rapid evolution or else extinction due to natural causes, or there may have been an invasion of Europe by new types of man who eliminated Neanderthalers by the sword or by interbreeding. However, the stone implements manufactured by human beings changed too: the Mousterian 'industry' gave way to the Upper Palaeolithic.

As these changes were taking place, *Equus hemionus* entered Europe and replaced *Equus hydruntinus*, which hung on only in Italy, Sicily, and south-eastern Europe. The newcomers were as far as one can tell similar to medium-sized onagers such as the kulan, but not enough is known of them for a detailed comparison. Upper Palaeolithic man painted on his cave walls amazing representations of the animals familiar to him, and among these appear a few onagers: both as fossils and frescoes, however, onagers are much less abundant than wild horses.

Equus hydruntinus, meantime, remained in the Mediterranean area: even after the Ice Age was over it continued to exist for some time, and its remains are known from Elba, several sites in Sicily and Italy, as well as in Rumania, some being as late as Neolithic. But gradually it died out, and it seems logical to suppose that the spread of domesticated horses and asses in Europe had something to do with this. Neither *Equus hydruntinus* nor *Equus graziosii*, it should be noted, are ancestral to living species of ass. Outside Europe, fossil remains of asses are very few and far between. The remains of *Equus africanus palestinae* have already been mentioned; remains of *Equus africanus africanus* have recently been uncovered from prehistoric Nubia and claimed in the middle Pleistocene of Algeria; and at several sites in the

Middle East as far east as Anau in Turkmenia remains of onagers occur which may well have been domesticated (a subject to be discussed in Chapter 5). But so far the only late Pleistocene asses known in Asia are *Equus hemionus ordosensis*, described from one adult and two juvenile skulls from the upper Pleistocene of Sjara-Osso-Gol on the Hwang-Ho in Kansu; and *Equus hemionus nipponicus* from Japan. Today the Ordos desert is far too arid even for a wild ass, but is not far from the Gobi where *Equus hemionus luteus* is found. Indeed, the Ordos race seems very similar to the Gobi dziggetai, but is much smaller: the size of a ghor-khar or less.

Although they are so common in the late Pleistocene of Europe, ass remains are scarce earlier in the Pleistocene. A few remains ascribed to *Equus hydruntinus* have been found in Europe, and from deposits at least half a million years old in India come the skulls of the onager-like species *Equus sivalensis*. In the early Pleistocene, over a million years ago, of the Val d'Arno in Italy occur the remains of *Equus stehlini*, so far the earliest known ass; it occurs alongside late representatives of *Equus stenonis* (for which see Chapter 1), and was only recently distinguished from it, since it is a very primitive type: but features like the prominent post-orbital bars of the skull, and the high narrow hooves, make it plain that it was indeed a wild ass.

In America, on the other hand, asses seem to have flourished from about a quarter of a million years ago, almost to the present day. Probably a species as close to the onager as to the African wild ass entered the New World about this time or a little earlier, and became widespread in the deserts of Mexico and the southern United States. The common species throughout this time was *Equus conversidens*, a very small form with rather short, broad cannon bones; several other species have been described but they all seem to be variants of the same form. The later representatives of this species, *Equus conversidens littoralis*, became even more dwarfed in size and may be the smallest type of the genus *Equus* that there has been: certainly under a metre high.

Quinn described a number of species of equid from the middle and upper Pleistocene of North America, some of which he claimed were specifically allied to onagers, because they had long, slender cannon bones unlike the short broad ones of *Equus conversidens*; and he associated with these cannon bones some isolated teeth which seemed to resemble onagers. It has been found, however, that whenever these slender limb-bones can be found associated with skulls and teeth they belong not with the onager-like teeth (which are probably in the main just variants of horse and *conversidens* teeth), but with species of the peculiar subgenus *Amerhippus*, the horses that quite lacked the incisor infundibulum. This is unexpected, because the South American species of *Amerhippus* had short broad limbs, and so did their immediate ancestor in North America, *Equus occidentalis* which survived until the last Ice Age or even after; but the two earlier species, the small *Equus fraternus* and the large *Equus complicatus*, which lived in interglacial times, none the less were slender-limbed. Probably it is just that short, broad shanks are more suited to cold climates.

4 Zebras

Zebras, as everyone knows, are striped horses. But there is more to them than that. As we found in Chapter 1, they are the most primitive living equids; their skulls and teeth closely resemble those of the earliest single-toed equids, and even their limbs show this. It has recently been shown that if we take the length of the cannon bones (metacarpals) and compare them to the length of the shannon bones (metatarsals), the value in zebras is higher than in horses or asses: in other words, zebras have longer front legs than other equids. The metacarpal to metatarsal ratio is 83–5 per cent in horses and African wild asses, 85–7 per cent in onagers, but 87–90 per cent in zebras. In the early single-toed horses like *Equus stenonis* and *Equus robustus* the values are also high—87–90 per cent, as in zebras.

Moreover, it can be shown that the zebras are not a uniform group: one species, Grévy's zebra, stands on its own. Its long, narrow skull and the pattern of its cheekteeth show that it is in many ways a little-changed descendant of these early equids; while the remaining species of zebra are more closely related to the horses and asses. So Grévy's zebra is put in a subgenus, *Dolichohippus*, along with these early horselike forms, while the others are separated into their own subgenus, *Hippotigris*. The two subgenera were already separate well over a million years ago.

BURCHELL'S ZEBRA

The zebra we see most commonly in zoos, and the one most widely distributed in Africa, is Burchell's zebra (*Equus* (*Hippotigris*) *burchelli*); also called the plains zebra and the bontequagga. This plump little animal is found all over east and south-east Africa and in to the south-west. The prominent German ethologist, Hans Klingel, who has studied them very intensively, estimates that there are about 300,000 of them living in the wild, but their population is not evenly spread. The Serengeti–Mara plains, east of Lake Victoria in Tanzania and Kenya, is their prime habitat, and here two-thirds of the total are concentrated.

A Burchell's zebra stands about 105–35cm at the withers; those found in southern Africa, south of the Zambesi, are larger than those of East Africa (135cm, against 125cm). A good stallion will weigh about 300kg. Always fat and sleek in appearance, he is rather dumpy and short-legged; his hooves are rather broad like a horse's; and his mane, crisp and upstanding—continuing the stripes of the neck.

The colour pattern is basically similar in all Burchell's zebras, but differs quite markedly in its detail. In the East African race, known as Grant's or Böhm's zebra, the stripes are broad and dark and stand out sharply against the white ground-colour. The stripes are vertical on the neck and body, but begin to bend back halfway along the flanks, so that those on the haunches are horizontal and continue like this down the back legs. The stripes meet under the belly and go right down to the hooves.

The Burchell zebras of Zambia—east of the Muchinga Escarpment—and Malawi, as well as that part of Mozambique north of the Zambesi river, are a little different from Grant's race, being more intensely striped, with both stripes and interspaces being much narrower. This race is known as Crawshay's zebra. West of the Muchinga Escarpment, as well as in neighbouring areas of

Page 125   *Kulan on Barsa Kelmes, an island in the Aral Sea. Though introduced to this island, the herd has an ideal habitat—dry wormwood scrub and desert*

Page 126 (above) *Kulan during the rut, in Badkhys Reserve. The stallion (second from the right) is rounding up gravid mares, and will cover them soon after they have given birth;* (below) *the Dziggetai of northern Mongolia,* Equus hemionus hemionus, *in May during the moult. This race, although still fairly numerous, is little known and not often photographed·*

Angola and the Congo, the Upper Zambesi race is found, which more resembles Grant's zebra but differs in its skull.

South of the Zambesi the picture changes. Instead of being white, the ground-colour in these zebras is buff; the mane is much better developed; the legs are usually not completely striped; and between the main stripes on the haunches are paler, narrower stripes known as shadow-stripes. Some zebras north of the Zambesi have very indistinct shadow-stripes (except for Crawshay's, which never does), but they are never as numerous or well-marked as those in the southern zebras. In fact, in some of the southern zebras there are even shadow-stripes on the neck.

As we go south, the Burchell zebras south of the Zambesi become less and less striped, the stripes getting wider apart again and, as it were, receding up the legs. Chapman's zebra, the form of Burchell's zebra found in Rhodesia, north-east Botswana, and southern Mozambique, has limited shadow-stripes, fairly narrow striping on the hindquarters, and broken stripes on the shanks. The Damara zebra (also known as Wahlberg's), which occurs as far south-east as Natal and as far north-west as southern Angola, has broader haunch-stripes with well-marked shadow-stripes, and the leg-stripes do not reach farther down than the knees and hocks. Finally the typical Burchell's zebra, now extinct, had completely white legs striped only to the elbow and stifle, and the stripes did not reach the midline of the belly.

This picture may seem confusing, but it is simple in outline. First, there is a distinct break across the Zambesi: some people have suggested that the northern and southern forms are distinct species. Certainly the differences are very great, for instance those north of the Zambesi alone among living equids almost always lack an infundibulum in the lower incisors whereas those south of it possess at least a trace; but there is no indication of any species difference. Secondly, there is the cline (gradual geographic change) in stripe density: those with the narrowest striping are found along the lower Zambesi, and the stripes get broader to

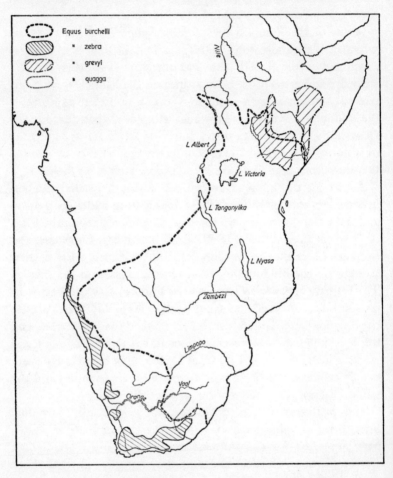

Fig 8   *Distribution c 1800, of the four species of zebra*

the north, south and west of there. Thirdly, there is the cline of stripe reduction south of the Zambesi, with the stripes gradually receding up the legs and disappearing from the belly.

It has already been pointed out that East African races have shorter, scruffier manes than southern ones. This condition reaches its peak in the entirely maneless zebras that are found on the north-eastern and north-western edges of the range: in Somalia, along the Juba river, and again in a district from the Karamojong region of Uganda into the southern Sudan. In the Somali population all adults are maneless, but in the Sudan–Uganda population there appear to be maned females. Always, however, the foals have manes; it has been found that in captive animals the mane is shed at sexual maturity, and in maneless zebras it simply fails to re-grow. Maneless zebras appear to have white (unstriped) ears, and other differences have been suggested—they may, for example, have more completely striped tails; they may or may not represent a separate geographic race, but since manelessness crops up sporadically throughout East Africa it is not strictly localised.

Distribution of Burchell's zebra

Where do Burchell's zebras live, and how do they live? Formerly, the species occurred as far south as the upper Orange river and Natal, but farther west it was absent from Namibia except for the northern strip. It lived in eastern and northern Botswana, southern and south-eastern Angola, Rhodesia, Mozambique, Zambia, Malawi, the south-eastern part of Zaire, Tanzania; in Kenya, everywhere except the extreme north-eastern corner which is too arid for it; in southernmost Somalia; in the lowlands of south-western Ethiopia, up the Rift Valley as far as Lake Zwai; in southern and north-eastern Uganda; and in the Sudan along the east bank of the Nile as far north as Shambe, where it occurs locally on the west bank also. Today, however, it is quite gone from the southern part: there are none left in Cape Province, the

Orange Free State, most of the Transvaal and Natal, and much of Botswana. The southernmost remaining populations are the small, isolated one in Zululand, and the large one in the Etosha Pan National Park, Namibia. In the north, however, the range today is much the same as it always was, but there are fewer animals.

Reintroductions have been made over parts of the former range in the Transvaal; but no one can bring back the typical Burchell's zebra, with its white legs and unstriped belly, which has disappeared for ever.

Herd organisation of Burchell's zebra

The Burchell's zebra herd consists of a family group, a stallion with from 1–6 mares and their offspring: up to 16 animals in all. Within the herd is a rank order: the stallion takes precedence, then the mares in order, then the young. The stallion is, however, somewhat peripheral; he may keep at some distance from the rest of the herd, and movements seem to be directed by the leading mare.

The herd is very stable; the animals recognise each other, and when a member is missing they search for it. Several herds may aggregate together in rich grazing areas, at night, or during migrations when thousands may be on the move together; but always when the big groups split up the subgroups are found to have the same membership. Klingel found that removing the stallion did not affect the cohesiveness of the herd; a new stallion would generally come along, and take over the mares and foals as a whole.

The surplus males, usually youngsters not yet in possession of their own herds, live together in a bachelor band of up to 15 animals. These groups, too, tend to be stable. Some males prefer to live solitary lives. The young males leave their herds at between 1 and 3 years to join a bachelor band: usually it is at the end of the first year when the mother has a new foal, but some

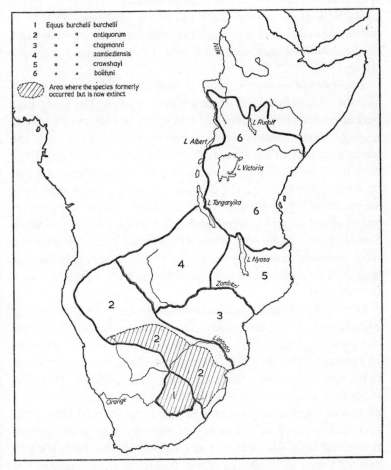

1   Equus burchelli burchelli
2   "   "   antiquorum
3   "   "   chapmanni
4   "   "   zambeziensis
5   "   "   crawshayi
6   "   "   boëhmi

Area where the species formerly
occurred but is now extinct

Fig 9   *Distribution in former times and today of Burchell's zebra*

remain in the herd for up to 4 years, especially if there are other youngsters in the group which can act as playmates. But, be it noted, there was no antagonism between the maturing males and the herd stallion: they were not driven out of the herd, but simply left it.

The fate of young females is different. When only 13–15 months old, a female first comes into oestrus. The early heat periods are not accompanied by ovulation, but the female adopts a typical oestrus stance which attracts young males outside the herd. These disturb the herd; the herd stallion challenges them, usually to no effect because of their superior numbers, and one of them abducts the young female. The young mare then lives an unsettled life, constantly changing hands, but as she matures her youthful oestrus stance becomes less conspicuous, and when this happens—at about 2 years of age—she will stay with the male with whom she happens to be. It is only after this that she begins to ovulate, and so it is that foals are born only into ready-formed herds.

Most foals—over 85 per cent—are born between October and March, with a peak in January. The gestation period is 371 days on average; oestrus follows only a few days after foaling, as in horses, so that a female has a chance to become pregnant in two successive years. However, since the gestation period is more than one year, the post-partum oestrus gradually gets out of phase, so that the chances of breeding in successive years become less and less: in fact in Ngorongoro over 40 per cent of mares foal only one year in three, one-third give birth for two years in three, and only 15 per cent foal three years running. Ten per cent of the mares in Klingel's three-year sample never gave birth at all. The foals can get up within the hour, and run around shortly after that. The sex ratio at birth is 85 males to 100 females, and this seems to persist approximately into adulthood, although there does seem to be—as in horses— a higher mortality for young males.

Habitat of Burchell's zebra

The herds are not territorial: that is to say, they do not have a piece of ground which they defend against other herds. They are, however, sedentary to the extent that they occupy a definite home range. In the Ngorongoro Crater this home range is from 30–100 or more square miles (80–250km²), over which the herd wanders; most of this area is also part of the home range of other herds. In the Serengeti, home ranges are larger, 300–400km² in the rainy season; in the dry season they migrate for 100–50km, and occupy dry season ranges as much as 600km² larger than rainy season ones.

The typical habitat of Burchell's zebra is a flat open plain, grassy or at least with sufficient ground vegetation to sustain a grazing animal. Zebras will eat old grasses which are too rank and coarse for most antelopes; this, together with the fact that they have preferred foods which antelopes do not favour, permits them to coexist with many species of antelopes in the same area. In particular, they seem to graze alongside the brindled gnu (also known as the blue wildebeest); herds of the two are often seen intermingled, although when the animals take to flight they separate again. In the Kruger National Park it has been found that two-thirds of zebra herds are seen in association with other species—most of these (45 per cent of the total) were with gnu.

Klingel studied the family life of Burchell's zebras all over Africa: in the Ngorongoro Crater, on the Serengeti Plains, in the Kruger National Park, the Etosha Pan Game Reserve (Namibia) and the Wankie National Park, Rhodesia. The herd structure is very much the same in all these places, differing only slightly: for example, herds tended to be larger in Ngorongoro than elsewhere, averaging 7·05 individuals and having as many as 16 in one herd; in Serengeti the average was only 5·1, and in the other three localities, 4·5–4·7. Basically, these differences depended on the number of mares—an average of nearly 3 mares per herd in

Ngorongoro, and only 2·2 in Serengeti. The bachelor bands, too, varied in size, averaging 3 individuals in Kruger, but only 1·6 in Etosha because of the high frequency of solitary stallions here.

The five areas studied had vastly different rainfall figures, from 907·5mm annually in Ngorongoro down to 323mm in Etosha. This seemed to be reflected in the figures for foal survival: at the beginning of the breeding season, Klingel found that in Ngorongoro 48 per cent of mares still had foals of the previous season, whereas in Etosha only 14 per cent of mares did; the other populations varied between these extremes, in the same order as their rainfall figures. This meant that in Etosha there was a much higher turnover, and many mares bred for several years running, losing each foal in succession until they struck lucky and one survived. It is possible, at the other end of the scale, that the survival figures in Ngorongoro (and also in Serengeti) were unnaturally high in the years when Klingel studied them (1964–5) for, as he notes, the previous years had been unusually dry, and the two populations were probably rebuilding their numbers after a heavy mortality. Certainly in Ngorongoro only about a 5 per cent foal mortality was detected; by the end of the breeding season, fully half the mares had foals which had survived the crucial early weeks.

What happens to these unfortunate foals that fail to survive? Many are taken by lions, hyaenas and wild dogs; others simply get lost and starve to death; and perhaps some die of disease. A short while ago, I found one of these foals in thorn-bush country on the right bank of the Tana river, in Kenya. A group of us were driving up the dirt road, and noticed vultures sitting on a clump of acacias to our left, others wheeling and soaring in the sky above. We stopped the Land Rover, got out and walked into the bush, ready all the time to retreat if it was a lion's kill: but there, lying alone, was the body of a zebra foal, just starting to stiffen, without a mark on it. What had it died of? We could not say: as we had other business in hand we could not stop to investigate, and left the sad remains to the vultures and marabous.

In the Kaokoveld, of northern Namibia, Burchell's zebras frequently climb hills, although they seem to prefer flat or undulating country. They are fond of sandbaths, which they roll in like horses, with their legs in the air. When feeding, the herd walks upwind, spread out; they are easily stampeded and put to flight, and in this respect are the most wary of the plains grazers.

It has been described how Burchell's zebras will react with antagonism to donkeys; they may trot within 80 yards of waggons drawn by donkeys; and they collect outside kraals, calling back and forth to the donkeys who then try to break out. If they do, the zebras chase them, kicking and biting. Understandably, zebras have not been the favourite animals of settlers.

Social relations

The calls of Burchell's zebras seem to differ according to locality. Those of southern Africa make a sound represented as 'qua-ha, qua-ha'—the origin of the Hottentot word 'quagga'. From a distance the sound is said to sound like wild geese honking. Grant's zebra of East Africa, however, has a rather different sort of call, a deep hoarse grunt varied by a short whistle.

Burchell's zebras greet each other, like horses, with pricked-up ears, sniffing at different parts of each others bodies, especially the nostrils, neck, withers, flanks and tail. Grzimek found that their behaviour was just the same towards a stuffed zebra—even towards a rather poor painting of a zebra! This is interesting: it implies that, at least in the initial stages, visual cues are more important than scent ones in recognition. Certainly Klingel was under the impression that the members of a herd recognise each other by their stripe patterns, their scent, and also by their voices, which differ slightly from one individual to another. An interesting sidelight on the theme of sight recognition was provided by Grzimek's experiment on the zebras of the Ngorongoro Crater; at first they did not respond to the clean and bright stuffed zebra that was presented to them—they only showed the typical greeting behaviour after the model had been well and truly dirtied by rolling it in the dust!

This last finding leads to all kinds of speculation. If zebras— at any rate, Burchell's zebras—recognise only dust-laden individuals (the normal appearance, after all!) as belonging to their own species, then of course they would not recognise new-born foals as one of them, if the foals were bright black and white. Is this perhaps why the foals are in fact, for the first few weeks of life, not black and white but a shaggy-coated buff colour with brown stripes? Secondly: since Grévy's zebra and the mountain zebras are black and white, we may suppose that so were the ancestors of Burchell's zebra—so that Grant's race retains the ancestral colour, while the races south of the Zambesi have changed, since they keep a buff ground-colour throughout life at least on the body (the legs and belly, however, are white). This may be to ensure that a zebra is always recognised by its mates as a zebra, even though it may on occasion be clean, not dust-covered. Have the southern races of Burchell's zebra evolved then to look as if they are permanently dirty, for recognition purposes?

Fights between zebra stallions, like those between horses, are vicious affairs of biting and kicking. They certainly occur when young males are trying to steal a young filly from a herd, and may also occur between herd males. The herd male threatens with ears directed forward, the head stretched out in front with the mouth closed, then he raises his head higher; his mouth then opens wide with the lips pulled back, and his ears are laid back. If the rival is not intimidated, a fight follows. The two bite each other's throat, neck, foreparts, forelegs, mouth; they may stand side by side, circling each other, biting each other's hindlegs and trying to reach the scrotum—this type of fight may even take place with the animals sitting or lying down. They may turn back to back and lash out with their hind hooves. When finally one has had enough and wishes to submit, he turns his head down and sideways, but the opponent persists, showing his teeth and biting the other's shoulder; at last the victor lays his head along the loser's croup, and fighting ceases.

Burchell's zebra is the only species that is widespread in Africa. During the Pleistocene period it even occurred in Algeria; its remains have been long known from several sites there under the name of *Equus mauritanicus*, but it is the same species as the living Burchell's zebra. Even remains attributed to the African wild ass have turned out, on re-study, to belong to Burchell's zebra. This makes it all the more puzzling why there are no zebras today on the savannahs of West Africa; indeed there is only one small population found west of the Nile. Until we know more about the species' exact ecological requirements, this will remain a mystery.

MOUNTAIN ZEBRA

Much less abundant is the mountain zebra (*Equus* (*Hippotigris*) *zebra*) of South Africa. Thinner and sleeker than Burchell's zebra, with narrower more ass-like hooves, the mountain zebra differs in many small ways. The striping pattern differs: the belly is never striped, the stripes always stopping fairly cleanly on the lower flanks; the vertical body-stripes continue right back to the tail, above the broad bent-back haunch-stripes (this is often referred to as the 'grid-iron' pattern); the spinal-stripe is narrow and is joined by the body-stripes, whereas in Burchell's zebra it is broader and disconnected from them. The facial-stripes are not black but dark brown; those on the forehead are tan-coloured. On the middle of the throat is a small square dewlap, more conspicuous in the male. Curiously, too, the hair along the midline of the back, from croup to withers, grows forwards instead of backwards. The ears are long; the mane is high, erect, and better developed than most Burchell's zebras. There are differences, too, in the skull and teeth, although they do not amount to much. It has been found recently that the heart of a mountain zebra weighs 3·20kg, whereas that of a Burchell's zebra of the same size weighs only 2·05kg: an obvious adaptation to living in a mountain environment.

Habitat

Mountain zebras formerly occurred throughout the mountain ranges of southern and western Cape Province, and up the west coast through the desert ranges of the Namibian coast in to Angola, where its range stops about 130km north of Mossamedes. Today, the northern part of the range, north of the Orange river, remains more or less intact although, as with Burchell's zebra, the populations are much thinned out; but in the southern part, in Cape Province, the mountain zebra has today become restricted to just a very few isolated areas.

Subspecies of mountain zebra

The species is divided into two subspecies, easily recognisable. The northern part of the range is occupied by the race known as Hartmann's zebra; the southern part, by the Cape mountain zebra. Hartmann's is a larger animal, 130cm high; the Cape form is only 120cm, making it the smallest of living zebras. Hartmann's has an off-white ground-colour with fairly narrow, widely spaced stripes; the Cape race has a pure white ground-colour with broad black bands close together, so that the stripes are broader than the spaces between them. The Cape form is altogether a more stockily built animal with even narrower hooves, and rather longer ears, and a larger dewlap. There is also a rather weakly marked cline of colour within the range of Hartmann's zebra: those in the northern part of its range—Angola and Kaokoveld—tend to be a more faded buff white, with blackish-brown stripes and a deep brown muzzle whereas those to the south are brighter, almost ochre-yellow, with black stripes and a dark grey muzzle. These are only average differences and are not as great as those that separate the Cape and Hartmann's races, and no further subspecies are usually recognised.

Where the ranges of the two forms met is disputed. According to some suggestions, Hartmann's zebra ranged south of the Orange river in to Little Namaqualand and the Kamiesberg; in the view of others, the boundary between the two was at the lower Orange river itself—between Great and Little Namaqualand, the present-day political units of Cape Province and Namibia. Unfortunately, there are no specimens from that region to settle the point; and there are no zebras living there today. However, Otto Antonius, the great hippologist of the first half of this century, found that early records of zebras from the mountains near Cape Town seemed to describe animals that were as large as Hartmann's but resembled the Cape form in colour; and Lundholm in 1952 described a subfossil skull from Vanwycksfontein, not far south of the Orange, as a new race *Equus zebra greatheadi*, of the size of Hartmann's zebra but differing in minor details. Probably this is the answer: the intervening area was inhabited by an intermediate race.

Ecological behaviour of mountain zebras

Klingel has found that the social life of the mountain zebra is on exactly the same lines as that of Burchell's. The herd travels in single file along the mountain tracks, the stallion in the lead (whereas the Burchell herds are always led by the lead mare); he mounts small hillocks to survey the countryside and signals all clear with a neigh; and he is said to drink last when the herd comes to a waterhole. Hartmann's zebra, at least, has a greater ability to go without water than Burchell's; the herd may drink every three days or so, and the animals often dig for water in dry river beds, down for nearly two feet, and other animals often take advantage of the water found in this way. The environment inhabited by Hartmann's zebra is a dry, scrubby semi-desert, and one with little shade; the zebras seek out thorn-bushes to lie up in the noonday sun.

Over most of its range, Hartmann's zebra is the only zebra found; but in Kaokoveld and south-west Angola (where, unlike farther south, it occurs as much as 100 miles inland) it occurs alongside Burchell's zebra. The densities of the two species change: in the west, Hartmann's zebra is more common, but becomes scarcer towards the east as Burchell's increases in abundance. Careful observers have made interesting comparisons between the two species in the Kaokoveld. Hartmann's zebra moves more freely than Burchell's, in a less lumbering gallop, with its head held high and nearly horizontal, the neck arched backwards; after an initial gallop it settles down to a trot and—unlike Burchell's—does not stop to look back when in flight, not at least for a considerable distance. When in flight, too, Hartmann's zebra makes for the hills. Herd sizes are exactly the same as in Burchell's zebra of Etosha Pan, although fewer stallions are solitary. No social grooming seems to occur in the herd: in strong contrast to Burchell's.

The flesh of Hartmann's zebra is said to be fine-grained with white fat and sinews; that of Burchell's is coarse, rank and dark red with yellow fat and sinews. Unlike Burchell's zebra, Hartmann's zebra show no tendency at all to associate with other species—gnu, ostrich or anything else. The calls of both races of mountain zebra have been well described as 'a low snuffling neigh or whinny', quite unlike that of Burchell's zebra which, according to Shortridge, a zoologist who was familiar with both in their natural habitat, sounds hysterical by comparison.

Hybrids between Burchell's and mountain zebra have been bred in captivity. They resembled Burchell's zebra more closely except for the larger ears and the pattern of the hindquarters and they lack the dewlap of the mountain zebra. They seem to be sterile.

Past and present status of mountain zebras

Although still found over most of its former range, Hartmann's zebra cannot be described as secure. The total world population has been estimated at between 5,000 and 8,000; like most equids, however, it breeds well in captivity; of the 90 specimens (29 males, 61 females), 37 have been born there. In 1960, there were 10,700, and in the 1950s, 50,000–75,000. The cause of this catastrophic decline is competition from domestic stock; this arid area is used by white farmers, although entirely unsuitable as farmland, and because of the land's marginal status, competition between wild and domestic animals is all the more severe. The farmers regard the zebras as vermin and shoot them (all too often, with government permission). Of the 5,500 Hartmann's zebras in Namibia, only a third are found in areas which are afforded any degree of protection.

The Cape mountain zebra, by contrast with Hartmann's, is very rare indeed; it must be ranked as one of the most severely endangered forms of large mammals. Formerly it occurred on all the ranges of southern Cape Province, from Cape Town in the west to Cathcart in the east, and the Steynsburg district in the north. Today it occurs on just a few of them.

In 1922 there were still thought to be over 400 Cape mountain zebras remaining: 330 of them on farms in George district, 50 on farms in Oudtshoorn, 20 on a farm in Sutherland, and 27 on mountains in the Cradock district. In 1937 a census showed just 20 in the Oudtshoorn district and 25 in the Cradock area. It was decided that the remainder needed protection, and the Mountain

Zebra National Park was declared at Cradock in that year. That the mountain zebra needed protection was undeniable, but the choice of location for the park was unrealistic, for a survey in that year showed it contained just 5 stallions and one mare. By 1947 the stallions were down to two, and the mare died in that year. On 22 August 1950 the two stallions were shot and their remains given to the Transvaal Museum. So the Mountain Zebra National Park contained no mountain zebras.

In the same year, however, in November, Mr H. J. Lombard presented the 11 mountain zebras which lived on his farm at Waterval, also in the Cradock district, to the National Parks Board, and they were placed in the National Park. (In view of this, the shooting of the previous two stallions must be considered a rather mistaken action, even if understandable at the time.) In 1956, their number had increased to 17; by 1960 they had reached 25. Next to the National Park is a farm owned by Mr N. D. C. Michau, at Doornhoek, which in 1960 contained 43 animals, having grown from a mere 7 in 1922. In 1964 this herd was donated to the National Park.

Between 1967 and 1969, the South African zoologist, J. C. G. Millar, made a complete survey of all areas where Cape mountain zebras were known to exist, or might still exist but have been overlooked. He found that a surprising number of very small populations still remained in isolated mountainous regions: 16 (6 males, 8 females, 2 young) in the Kammanassie range, 7 (3 males, 3 females, 1 young) in the Kouga range, 3 in the Outeniqua range, and 13 (5 males, 8 females) in the Gamka mountains. This was in addition to those found in protected areas—namely those in the National Park at Cradock, now 98 in number, and 3 in the De Hoop Provincial Wildlife Farm, Bredasdorp district. This makes a total of 140, of which 39 were living outside protected areas. Millar pointed out that those in the unprotected areas had declined from an estimated 135 in 1937, whereas those in protected areas had risen from 25 in the same year. The conclusion

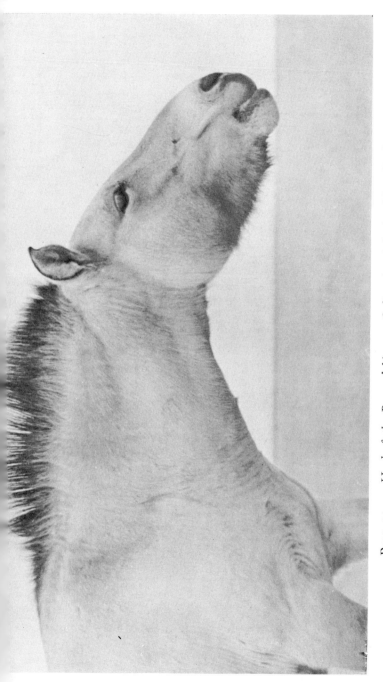

Page 143   Head of the Przewalski mare Orlitsa in Askaniya Nova Park, Ukraine. Captured in 1947 in the Takhin-Shara-Nuru mountains of the Mongolian Altai, she is the last specimen definitely recorded in the wild

Page 144 (above) *Maneless zebra shot on the lower Juba river, Somalia;* (below) *Nubian wild asses in the Catskill Game Park, New York State*

was obvious: those remaining outside protected areas must be translocated to safety. Millar has recommended that a reserve be created in the Gamka mountains, and that all the members of the other three unprotected groups should be captured by tranquillising them, and transferred to Gamka.

The zebras of Cradock

Hans Klingel, who has taught us almost all we know about the family life of zebras, studied the mountain zebras of Cradock in 1965. Their general social system, he found, is like that of Hartmann's zebra and therefore not too different from Burchell's zebra. In 1965 there were 55 zebras in the reserve, divided into 9 family herds, averaging 4·5 members each (one stallion, 1–4 mares, and foals), and one bachelor band of 6 individuals. Only one member of the bachelor band was adult; the others were maturing males. A 2-year-old male moved several times between his family herd and the bachelor band; it seems that here was a male in the process of leaving his herd and as in Burchell's zebra there was no trace of antagonism between him and the herd stallion, his presumed father.

In 1967 Klingel returned to Cradock to see what changes had occurred; the population had meantime increased to 69, and there were quite marked changes in the social structure, which could be pinpointed the more easily because of the characteristic, recognisable stripe pattern of each individual. The family herds now averaged 6·3 individuals, and there were now two bachelor bands with 8 and 4 members respectively. One herd stallion had died; two herd stallions, as well as one from the group of bachelors, had been captured for Pretoria zoo and Swellendam Reserve. The three herds thus deprived of their stallions had been taken over whole: two by stallions from the bachelor group, the third by a young male (not apparently from within the same herd), not yet mature in the 1965 survey. A change had taken place in a

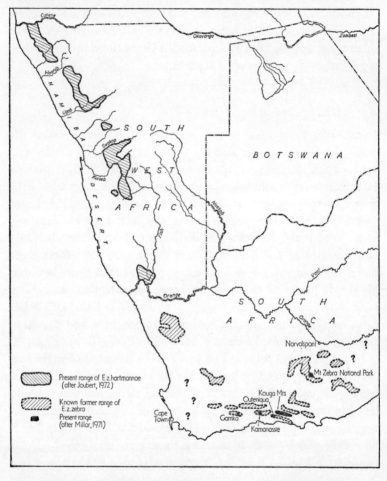

Fig 10 *Known range of* Equus zebra, *the mountain zebra*

fourth family herd, too: a male from among the former bachelors was now leading it, and the former herd stallion had become a bachelor. What equine drama had accompanied this unexpected event, we can only imagine.

Of the females, two that were formerly immature had grown up and left their herds, and joined others—doubtless having been abducted in the fashion described earlier for Burchell's zebra. Of five males that had been subadult in 1965, there was of course the lucky youngster that had taken over a family herd, while the other four had joined the bachelor groups. Unfortunately, it is not reported whether they now formed the group of four, or whether fission had occurred in the previous band.

The isolated herds of mountain zebras

The herd structure of the remaining groups (outside Cradock) is also very interesting. Millar found that altogether in the Kammanassie, Kouga and Gamka areas there were 9 herds: 4 consisting of 1 male and 1 female (of these, 2 also had youngsters), 2 consisting of 1 male and 2 females, 3 consisting of 1 male with 3 females (of these, one had a youngster). There were also 5 lone males (one being in a district of the Kouga range all by himself; one associating with a herd of 8 feral donkeys) and 2 lone females (one whose mate had recently died and was now alone in an isolated area, and one which was fenced in, mated with a donkey). Two neighbouring herds in the Kammanassie range had home ranges 3 miles apart, centred on permanent waterholes, with well-worn tracks and rolling places; the 2 herds in the Kouga range appeared to have non-overlapping home ranges, and when these herds met there was much vocalising and the male of the larger herd attacked the other.

The cry of the Cape mountain zebra is described by Millar as a whinny followed by a honk: this seems to be a difference from Hartmann's, although the two have not been analysed—

indeed, no one appears to have heard both of them to compare them!

THE DEMISE OF THE SOUTH AFRICAN FAUNA

The fauna of southernmost Africa was always rather different from that of the rest of the sub-Saharan area. Unfortunately, the early European settlers were unappreciative of it, so today very little remains. Boer farmers and trekkers would take their waggons on to the veldt and simply blaze away, picking up the dead animals to give meat to their Hottentot servants, leaving the wounded to die. It is difficult to realise that today's rolling farmlands and empty plains were once teeming with wildlife. Most of it was gone by 1850; too late a few farmers began to look around them at the last remnants and rounded them up to try to save them for posterity. But for the action of these public-spirited individuals the Cape mountain zebra would be extinct today; so would the white-tailed gnu, the bontebok, the blesbok, the red hartebeest and others. All of these became extinct in the wild and were preserved only on private farms. But they were too late to save the Cape lion, the Cape rhinoceros, the blaauwbok, and the quagga.

It is interesting to reflect that in East Africa there are still plenty of large mammals outside the reserved areas; in South Africa, there are none. East Africa certainly has its rarities, but it is only in South Africa that species have been totally exterminated.

QUAGGA

Early explorers spoke enthusiastically of a zebra-like animal called the quagga, a creature of beauty and speed. The explorer Sparrmann in the 1770s saw them on the southern coastal plain with bontebok and blaauwbok. Paterson, in 1777–9, saw them together with mountain zebras in the hinterland behind Algoa Bay. Levaillant in 1793 found them in Namaqualand, again with zebras. Sir John Barrow between 1795 and 1802 saw quaggas and zebras together in the Geelbeck-Fontein district of the south-western Great Karroo: the zebras were in a small herd, the quaggas in a large one. The quagga, he said, was very tame; the zebra on the other hand was rather savage.

In 1820 the Reverend John Campbell met a herd of more than 100 quaggas migrating south in the Orange river district near Ramah; every year, they went from the northern highlands of the Kunana district to winter around Mafeking where it is lower in altitude and milder. But already the big herds had been much depleted. Quaggas Flats, along the Great Fish river, had been named for its abundant quaggas, but by 1823, according to Thomson, there was no game at all except for a few elephants.

The last known wild quaggas were shot near Aberdeen in 1858 and Kingwilliamstown in 1861. It is possible, however, that a few survived on the plains south of the Vaal river until about 1878.

The shame of it is, that quaggas had been kept in captivity and survived well, but because no one imagined that a creature said to occur in such abundance could become extinct, no attempt was made to breed them. In the 1820s, a quagga was kept in the menagerie at Windsor Castle; in 1826, a phaethon drawn by a pair of 'horse-quagga' was the sensation of Hyde Park. One of these was doubtless the specimen painted by George Stubbs around 1820; the picture now hangs in the Royal College of Surgeons. About 1860, a team of quaggas drew the London zoo's forage waggon. The London zoo, in fact, had a whole series of quaggas one after the other; the last of them died in 1872. The last in the world died in Amsterdam zoo in 1883.

From time to time, supposed quagga survivals have hit the headlines. Someone claimed to have seen them in the Kaokoveld in 1913; in 1920, they were sighted in Ovamboland. Both these reports are very unlikely, as are others in that region: there is no likelihood that quaggas were ever found in northern Namibia, as the fauna is by now fairly well known and is in any case quite different from that of the Cape. Hartmann's zebra looks brownish from a distance and might be mistaken for a quagga; and this species, like Burchell's, sometimes abducts donkeys. A hybrid, between a donkey and a Hartmann's zebra which lived in Windhoek zoo was, according to Shortridge, striped on the foreparts only.

Quaggas are known to have occurred along the coasts of Cape Province as far east as the Great Kei river, and north as far as the Orange river in the west, but apparently crossing the Orange in the east into Orange Free State where it occurred as far north as the Vaal and north-east to the Winburg district. In the Orange Free State its range overlapped with that of Burchell's zebra; according to the artist-explorer Cornwallis Harris, the quagga associated in herds with the white-tailed gnu and the ostrich, while Burchell's zebra favoured the company of the brindled gnu.

Quaggas were essentially plains animals, although they occasionally wandered into hilly country. When alarmed they took off at a gallop, and though not as fast as Burchell's zebra, they surpassed it in endurance. The cry was a shrill barking sound, not dissimilar to the 'qua-ha' of Burchell's zebra; although the cry of the latter is obviously the origin of the name, quagga. Both then and now Burchell's zebras are also known as quaggas to many people—if a distinction is (was) made, the Burchell zebra is specified as bontequagga, meaning painted quagga.

The quagga was a little larger than the mountain zebra, about 132cm high; large-headed and small-eared like Burchell's zebra, but narrow-hoofed like the mountain zebra. Where it differed from both was in the striping, which was essentially confined to the head and neck. The dark stripes were brown rather than black, separated by cream or buff intervening spaces. The body was brown, the legs and belly white. (This may throw some light on the old question, 'are zebras white horses with black stripes, or black horses with white stripes?') The body-stripes gradually faded out along the flanks.

It has already been noted that the races of Burchell's zebra get less and less striped as they go south, and that the southernmost completely lacked stripes on the legs and belly. What more natural, thought many zoologists, than that the quagga should have been a still more southerly race with the stripes even more reduced? Although it seems reasonable at first sight this theory is no longer accepted. For one thing, there is clear evidence that quaggas and Burchell's zebras occurred together, without inter-breeding, in the Orange Free State—even, it seems, associating with different species of gnu. They were therefore reproductively isolated, as different species should be. Moreover, in those quaggas in which the body-stripes were tolerably distinct along the flanks, they showed no sign of beginning to bend back to form the Y-shaped 'saddle', characteristic of Burchell's zebra, between the upright and oblique stripes. There are differences, albeit slight, in both skull and teeth from Burchell's zebra: and these are about as much as one finds between Burchell's and mountain zebras. In general, the three species seem about equally interrelated; and all three occur as fossils at some sites, such as Kromdraai, in the Transvaal, which may be a million or more years old.

The known skins of quaggas—some twenty in number—differ quite considerably among themselves, and it has been suggested that there were a number of different geographic types or sub-species. Unfortunately few of the specimens have any definite locality closer than South Africa or, if we are lucky, the Cape, so it cannot be definitely known whether there was geographic variation or not. I would think not, on the whole; the most dis-tinctive of these supposed subspecies, which has been given the name *Equus quagga danielli* (the one with the most reduced striping of all, hardly extending behind the shoulders), is known from accurately localised skins, drawings and descriptions from places as far apart as the Winburg district (the farthest north-east locality known), the Fish river district in the south-eastern Cape, and Beaufort West in the west-central Cape. This leaves only a small area of the south-western Cape, around Cape Town itself, for the more fully striped races to have occurred in, and while the few localities known for such races—so-called *greyi* and *lorenzi*—are consistent, such as Stellenbosch and Steenbergen, there is really very little to go on. The late Austin Roberts, expert on South African mammals, noted that mammals found along the lower Orange river tend to be a pale colour, and suggested that a type of quagga called *isabellinus* (described as being pale coloured) was a distinct subspecies that lived in that district. But, intriguing as this is, there is still no real evidence either way!

Levaillant said that the Nama Hottentots, who live on either side of the lower Orange river, knew three kinds of zebra: *uri goreb* (white zebra), *ho goreb* (painted zebra), and *nu goreb* (black zebra). These are supposed to be, respectively, Burchell's zebra, Hartmann's zebra, and the quagga. He describes the two latter, saying that the quagga has a cry like a dog, and the Hartmann's zebra has a cry 'like a stone thrown hard on to ice'. As for Burchell's zebra, this is known to have lived as far south-west as Kuruman and Campbell, in northern Cape Province, north of the Orange river, but not known to have extended as far west as Great Namaqualand. Levaillant's evidence does at any rate indicate that they knew of its existence, and it is even possible that three species of zebra coexisted there.

GRÉVY'S ZEBRA

The three species—Burchell's zebra, mountain zebra, and quagga —are fairly closely interrelated: comparable, perhaps, to the three species of ass. But there is in Africa a fourth species of equid which, although it is called a zebra because it has stripes, is much more distantly related: Grévy's zebra, *Equus (Dolicho-hippus) grevyi*, the last representative of an ancient line, the first to split off from the equid stem after it became single-toed.

Grévy's zebra is the largest living wild species of equid, standing fully 150cm at the withers, and weighing some 400kg or more. Slenderly built, long-legged, and dazzlingly striped, Grévy's zebra is certainly the handsomest of the zebras. The stripes are very narrow and close together, black on white, but the belly is left clear white as in the mountain zebra, and so is a narrow zone on the croup either side of the broad black dorsal stripe. The pattern on the hindquarters is totally different from that of other zebras: instead of beginning to lie obliquely and finally horizontally, the flank-stripes begin to curve more and more with the concavity forwards; while the hindleg-stripes arch upwards and a third series of concentric arches spreads forwards and downwards from the tail. In this way, three arcs bend out and touch each other—an extraordinary and unique type of pattern.

The mane in this species is very tall and erect. The ears are extremely broad and furry inside; the facial-stripes are narrow, close together, and black. The hooves are fairly broad; the chestnuts (which like all zebras and asses are confined to the forelimbs) are extremely small and inconspicuous; and the splint bones—remains of the lateral metapodials—are long and clearly much less reduced than in other equids.

Many of these characters can be seen as very primitive; but most striking of all is the evidence of the skull. This is long and narrow, with a very narrow forehead and muzzle, and a long diastema; and the relatively small teeth, have thin enamel which is folded into a rather primitive pattern. The general impression closely resembles the ancient equids of $3\frac{1}{2}$–$2\frac{1}{2}$ million years ago—*Equus simplicidens*, *Equus robustus* and *Equus stenonis*. In fact the direct ancestor of Grévy's zebra, the almost identical *Equus plicatus* (known from South African fossil sites of about $2\frac{1}{2}$–1 million years ago), is very little different from *Equus robustus*, so that what we have essentially is a type of equid very similar to Grévy's zebra spread all over the Old World, and North America too, from which all other living equids are descended. This type hung on outside Africa until about 100,000 years ago in *Equus valeriani* of Teshik-Tash, in Samarkand; but today is found only in north-east Africa.

Habitat of Grévy's zebra

Grévy's zebra lives today in three countries: Kenya, Ethiopia and Somalia. In Kenya it is found only north of the Tana river, extending east about as far as Garissa and the Lorian swamp, and west to a line from Mount Kenya to Mount Nyiru and up the eastern side of Lake Rudolf. North of the Ethiopian border, its range extends up the eastern side of the Omo river, as far as Lake Zwai in the Rift valley south of Addis Ababa; to the east it does not extend much beyond Lake Stephanie, and is not found in Boran country farther east, although Burchell's zebra does occur there. In north-eastern Kenya the range ceases at, or near, the Ethiopian and Somali borders: in Somalia there are three rather isolated populations: in the rocky, chalky strip along the left bank of the Juba river between 2° and 3° 30′ N; in the Afmedo district; and on the eastern bank of the Webi Shebeli river near Gelib. From this last point the range extends into eastern Ethiopia, in the lowlands of Ogaden and Bale districts, but not into the mountains farther west nor into the desert farther north and east. The whole range thus forms a crescent with the two ends in Ethiopia and the middle in Somalia and Kenya.

Social organisation of Grévy's zebra

Klingel has studied Grévy's zebra, and finds its social organisation quite different from that of the mountain and Burchell's zebras. Instead of the cohesive herds of other equids, there are no permanent bonds between any two adult individuals. The stallions live in territories which they defend against rivals; these territories extend over 1–4 square miles (2·5–10km²) and are larger than those of any other grazing animal. A rival may be defined as any other stallion, so long as a female is present. That is to say, strange males are tolerated within a territory if no female, especially an oestrus female, is present; but as soon as an oestrus female sets foot within the territory, the strange males are driven off. The stallion tries to drive an oestrus female towards the centre of his territory, for other stallions respect the boundary. Fighting takes place only at the borders of the territories: inside them, no fighting occurs for the strange males are invariably submissive. If, for example, another male inadvertently enters the territory while an oestrus female is visiting, the owner will chase him out and he will not attempt to fight back. The territories are marked by small dungheaps, which the owner leaves at two or three spots along the borders and periodically adds to.

Females, in and out of oestrus, and males not showing territorial behaviour, may flock together in grazing groups, but they are not permanent and their composition may change within the hour. The animals migrate in search of water, and at this time, too, many individuals will be seen together. The mares, moving freely around as they do, are never found far from water; the territorial stallions tend to remain where they are, and migrate only if conditions become very severe. In the dry season, Klingel noticed that females often leave their young foals behind and walk off to drink. Foals may be left thus, quite unprotected, for a whole day! They must surely make easy prey at such times.

The phenomenon of territoriality, though widespread among mammals, is by no means universal. Of living equids, unless the incident of aggression described by Millar for Cape mountain zebras was territorial, only Grévy's zebra shows it; and only the males. A usual form of territoriality, seen among other mammals, is that a male, or a pair, or even a whole group, defend a small area at all times, the whole year round. Sometimes the males are territorial, but only at some seasons of the year: this occurs with some antelopes. Grévy's zebra is very unusual, perhaps unique, in that the males try to maintain territories all year round, but defend them only in the presence of females on heat: a kind of 'gentlemen's agreement' over a piece of ground. Keast, an American ecologist, found that, in Kenya, the male territories tended to be in dry rocky terrain, while the large grazing parties moved in flatter, scrubby country.

The gestation period is 390 days: by far the longest of any equid. Whether there is any special season of births is not known. The voice again is different from all other equids. It has been described as a very hoarse grunt, long drawn out, divided in the middle by a whistle with an apparent intake of breath.

GRÉVY'S AND BURCHELL'S ZEBRAS IN MIXED HERDS

Over much of the range of Grévy's zebra, Grant's race of Burchell's zebra is also found: to be specific, their ranges overlap over most of the western half of the Grévy crescent, from Lake Zwai down between Lakes Rudolf and Stephanie, south-east to Isiolo and Meru, and along the north bank of the Tana. To the east of Lake Stephanie, and in the eastern portion of the crescent, Grévy's zebra occurs alone; while elsewhere in Kenya, and in the Boran country of Ethiopia, Grant's occurs alone. In some areas of the overlap, such as the arid flat country round Baragoi and Wamba, Grévy's zebra is the commoner species; in the grasslands of the Leroghi plateau and Isiolo, Grant's is in the majority.

Where the two coexist, no hybrids are known, although mixed herds are very commonly formed. In the Isiolo/Uaso Nyiro region, in July, Allen Keast found that two-thirds of zebras were in mixed groups. Two of these groups were very large—160 and 250 animals, larger than groups of either would have been alone —and consisted of about three-quarters Grévy's, a quarter Grant's; others were much smaller, 15–20 animals, and in these Grant's outnumbered Grévy's by 3 or 4:1. Within each mixed group, the numerically inferior species tended to bunch into subgroups, especially when the group began to move, and kept towards the centre when the group took to flight. The mixed herds would graze in the morning at 1–2 miles from the river, rest under the trees at noon, and visit the river in the mid-afternoon, gradually moving away from it again as they grazed. Although in both species, especially in Grévy's, there was constant scuffling with animals biting each other and bickering, there was no aggression between members of the two species. Neither species was dominant, and there was no interspecific sexual activity.

One of the many interesting aspects of this arrangement is the comparison with the overlap zone between Burchell's and Hartmann's zebras in Kaokoveld. Here, there is no association between the two species; no mixed herds are formed. It may be that, as with monkeys so with zebras: distantly related species may associate together in mixed groups, but closely related species do not, at least as a rule. Perhaps the ease of interbreeding has something to do with it. As far as I know, no one has attempted to persuade Burchell's and Grévy's zebras to interbreed, but Grévy's and mountain zebras have done so, with difficulty; and Raymond Hook reports that there is an unusually high abortion rate of mares covered by Grévy's zebra stallions. On the other hand, Burchell's and mountain zebras hybridise with ease, although the hybrids are sterile. Perhaps the temptation would simply be too great for closely allied species!

5 Domestication

We all think we know what a domestic animal is, and we identify them as those animals which we keep in fields, pens or sweat-houses, feeding them at least part of the time, controlling their breeding so that they conform to type. They live largely for our well-being: giving us meat, milk, wool, transport, and companion-ship. We divide our domestic animals into those we *like*, on per-haps a rather anthropomorphic basis: these we pet and coddle, keep them fit, and give them names. The others we see as machines: we deny them individuality, and treat them harshly; sometimes, in fact, their ability to yield what we want from them depends on them being unfit, like geese reared for *foie gras*, or calves raised for veal. Horses and donkeys, like dogs and cats, tend to belong to the first group; cattle, sheep, pigs and chickens belong to the second. Either way, whether we cosset or imprison them, there is no doubt that they are domesticated.

Another indication of domestication is a division into distinct breeds. We all know what a dog is: but we would be hard put to define the dog by its physical characteristics at least in such a way as to distinguish it from the wolf. There is a far greater difference between a St Bernard and a Chihuahua than between a dog and a wolf. Much, though perhaps not all, of the differentiation within the dog has arisen by human activity, selecting certain individuals out of a litter to breed with others similar to them, and some breeds are notably different today from their ancestors at the turn of the century. All this is a matter of common practice, and the very origin of some breeds is a matter of historical record. But we have not by any means created distinct species; many a dog breeder has discovered to his annoyance that the prize cocker spaniel is totally uninterested in the stud male introduced to her at great expense, but prefers to jump over the gate and seek out the dreadful mongrel down the road.

Still, such enormous differences as exist between breeds of dogs cannot be ignored, and the question keeps cropping up, are they really all derived from a single stock? All dogs are certainly descended in one way or another from wolves; there is no wild canine that remotely resembles the Chihuahua with its bulbous forehead, the pug with its squashed nose, or the Pekinese with its poppy eyes, and by any reckoning such yapping extravagances have come a long way from the noble wolf that gave them birth. But this is not quite the point. When we endeavour to trace their antecedents, hypothesising about the very early stages of evolution—it is evident that they descend from different wolves. The British zoologist, Juliet Jewell, who has reconstructed the family tree of all domestic dogs by taking the common denominators of different breeds known to be related, considers that at least four different geographic races of wolf have been domesticated. Some of the lines have remained pure, others have been intercrossed; by selecting desirable characteristics for various purposes (which in many cases means merely emphasising the differences between the original four types of wolf), all modern breeds of dog have been derived.

The process is made much simpler by the existence of apparent intermediate stages of domestication. And it is here that we find that the western idea of domestication is not as simple as all that. In Assam there are cattle that live their lives free in the forest, but come to the villages to be fed, milked and slaughtered. There are donkeys in the Sahara that roam freely but are owned by different people who, when they move from place to place, recapture them, load them up and take them along—then release them at the next stopping-place. The dogs of villages in Africa, the Middle East and South-East Asia wander about the streets finding their own food, eating offal, breeding unrestrictedly; but they are willing and ready to help with hunting or herding when required, and indeed part of the reason why they are tolerated is because of the cleaning-up job they do. Are they domesticated? Most people would say yes; they are selected to do a job, but their breeding is very little controlled; they do work for man, but mostly live free.

A stage back from this is selective hunting. Reindeer hunters will follow specific herds; they know their movements, and depend entirely on them for their means of life. They kill selectively, too: they generally avoid killing females, and concentrate on non-breeding males, as they know that if they kill the stud bulls there will be fewer in the next generation. It is quite possible that such culling does improve the stock, and causes change analogous to domestication but in a much slower fashion. Or is it so analogous? More likely the relationship is more direct, and that it is from such roots that the intimate relationship we know as domestication gradually grew up. In line with this, we can notice that breeds of domestic animals are at different stages of differentiation: some are more, some less, like their ancestral wild stock. Some breeds of dog—the husky, the wolfhound—are much less altered from their ancestral wolves than most others.

In setting the scene, I have tried to avoid mentioning horses and asses, because of the controversies surrounding them. This is particularly true of horses. But the principles are the same: we have a variety of breeds of domestic horses and asses which differ strongly among themselves so that we cannot really differentiate a domestic type successfully from the wild types. This artificiality is the major reason why many zoologists no longer wish to use the names *Equus caballus* for the domestic horse and *Equus asinus* for the domestic ass: the names refer to mental constructs rather than to actual living species.

THE DOMESTICATION OF THE DONKEY

The story of the donkey is a much simpler one than the story of the horse, largely because there are many fewer breeds: they are mostly used for carrying loads, although breeding mules can be looked on as quite an important function. Wild asses are desert animals; and it is not surprising that donkeys are employed most widely in the arid areas of the world. There are very few breeds: the short-legged pygmy donkey of Sicily, the big white Egyptian donkey, the enormous black Poitou breed, and little else except an undifferentiated mass of ordinary donkeys. Most of these un-bred donkeys (ie not selected and bred for a specific task) are small (120cm or so in height), are grey with a light belly and white legs and muzzle, have cinnamon-coloured backs to the ears; a thin stripe along the spine, and a long bold cross-stripe over the shoulders. They have short sturdy limbs and very narrow hooves. The commonest variant on this is brownish-black instead of grey—a simple colour mutant. It is also notice-able that donkeys in the western Mediterranean region, especially Spain and Morocco, very often have at least traces of stripes on their legs.

The two living races of African wild ass have already been described. It seems to be generally agreed that the Somali wild ass has had little or no effect on the domestic ass: it is the wrong colour, wrongly marked, and differs in many skull features. Most people consider the Nubian wild ass as a better putative ancestor, and so it is: it has a more complete dorsal stripe, a better-marked shoulder-cross, a greyer colour and resembles the donkey in most skull features in which the Somali race differs. Even so, there are many differences: the shoulder-cross, even in the Nubian race, is not the boldly marked, long stripe of the donkey, and the backs of the ears are pale off-white rather than cinnamon. It is much larger, of course, and there are still differences in the skull. Of these different characteristics, I would think that only the smaller size of the ordinary grey donkey is likely to be due to domestication: people may choose smaller individuals to breed from as they are more manageable, but why should they select for, say, different-coloured ears? I am very dubious whether the Nubian wild ass can really be the ancestor of the donkey.

This leads us to conclude that the donkey must be derived from some kind of wild ass that is now extinct. Where do we know that there were wild asses formerly, but not today? As stated in Chapter 3, there is pictorial evidence of wild asses with both leg-stripes and a strong shoulder-cross from Algeria, and fossil evidence of a wild ass which was evidently domesticated *in situ* in Palestine; the latter being backed up by reports of wild asses—whether feral or truly wild, we do not know—in Arabia today. The Palestine ass is known only from teeth and limb-bones, and certainly it was a large animal, standing about 127cm at the shoulder, comparable to a Somali wild ass; this need not prevent it being the ancestor of the donkey, as remarked earlier. When we find skulls of this form, then we will know whether it could have been or not! As for the Algerian wild ass, the fact that it is the donkeys of the western Mediterranean that have the highest frequency of leg-stripes irresistably suggests that there may be some connection.

ONAGERS UNDER DOMESTICATION

Even though it is almost certain that a wild ass of African type—*Equus africanus palestinae*—was domesticated in Palestine, quite a different form was tamed in Mesopotamia by the Sumerians. The Syrian wild ass or onager, *Equus hemionus hemippus*, now extinct, was perhaps the earliest type of equid of all to be domesticated. There are remains of this little creature from Neolithic and early Bronze Age sites all over the Mesopotamian area, suggesting either that they hunted it a great deal or, more likely, that they kept them in captivity and used them for some special purposes. However, it is the artwork of the Sumerians which has supplied us with conclusive evidence. Not only have items such as a bronze bit in the form of an onager been discovered, but the famous Royal Standard of Ur even depicts onagers drawing chariots. At least, they are thought to be onagers: the tail is tufted like an ass, the ears are not as long as might be expected for a typical donkey, and there is no shoulder-cross, though the intricacy of the illustration is such that we might have expected it to be shown had there been one.

Several hundred miles to the north-east of Ur, at Anau in Turkmenia, a site also spanning late Neolithic and early Bronze Ages, we again find onager remains, and again in such abundance that it looks as if there was some form of domestication. The race represented at Anau is not the little Syrian race, but the larger kulan, which occurs in the area today.

All this evidence is significant for many reasons. First, it is interesting that the onagers of Ur are depicted as drawing chariots. They were used, therefore, for horselike purposes, not for donkey-like ones: they may of course have carried loads as well as pulling wheeled vehicles, but so far there is no evidence to suggest this. The usual interpretation is that there were no horses in Mesopotamia then; as we know, there were horses (either wild or domestic) in northern Mesopotamia in the first millenium BC for they are depicted at Nineveh, but there is no evidence for them earlier. So, it is thought, the Sumerians took what was available and made do. When horses arrived in the area, they were so much superior to onagers that onager-keeping was promptly dropped, and that, it is supposed, is why onagers are not domesticated to this day.

This is not totally true; onagers were until very recently—during World War II in India, for example—caught from time to time and crossed with either horses or, more usually (as in

Iran), with donkeys to make a kind of mule. These mules were certainly very hardy and strong, but often inherited the onagers' wild temperament. Even today along the border of the Rann of Kutch, people leave out their she-asses to be mated by onagers; the hybrids are said to be very strong and good load-carrying animals. They closely resemble Indian onagers except for the well-marked shoulder-stripe. Three of these hybrids can be seen in Ahmedabad zoo, obtained by its superintendent, Reuben David.

The domestication of onagers at Ur and Anau indicates that the domestication of a species does not have to spring from a single source, as some have maintained. Since the people of Anau obviously did not obtain their onagers by trade with Ur, for they are a different type altogether, it is probable that they followed the Chaldeans' example. The people of Palestine got the same idea, either from hearing about the Chaldeans or independently, and caught and trained their own local wild ass, which just happened to be a completely different species. And so donkey-breeding would have spread, by direct purchase and acquisition of donkeys from trading partners or by the spread of ideas rather than of the animals themselves, or even by independent invention. As time went by and international links increased, different peoples would come to know more and more about each other's domestic animals, and it would be found that the donkeys used in city A made the best pack animals, those bred in city B were the best for riding, and so on. Accordingly A and B would trade and exchange donkeys, so that each could have the best of both worlds; mostly, the two breeds would be kept separate for the special tasks at which each excelled, but there would be sure to be some bright spark who would experiment by crossing them to see whether the cross would combine both qualities or would excel at a third.

ORIGINS OF THE DOMESTIC HORSE

The history of ass-breeding and the speculations it produces are directly relevant to the much more complicated question of horse-breeding. The problem of the origin of domestic horses is much more similar to that of dogs than to that of donkeys, but the donkey principles can be used as a basis on which to build.

The first zoologist to make a special study of the origin of the horse—though Darwin had considered the matter in a general way—was the Frenchman, M. A. Sanson. He measured the skulls of domestic horses and divided them into two types, a long-headed and a short-headed; each of these was further divided into four species, which he saw as being the basic stocks from which domestic breeds have arisen. All his long-headed 'species' are varieties of heavy horses, and so is one of his short-headed types. The other three short-headed 'species' are called the Irish (which includes most ponies), the African (including the Barb and the Andalusian) and the Asiatic (including the Arab and general European riding horses). He gave them all names, but since they are all constructs—Platonic 'ideals' rather than actual animals—the names can have no standing in zoological nomenclature.

At the turn of the century Professor J. C. Ewart and Sir William Ridgeway both explored the matter. Ewart noted that among many breeds of Celtic ponies, such as Connemaras, Icelandic and Faeroese, there is a high frequency of aberrant features such as the absence of ergots under the fetlock, the lack of hock chestnuts, very small foreleg chestnuts, and a short-haired tail root like the Przewalski horse: features which are not seen in most other horse breeds at all. One-third of Faeroes ponies lack hock callosities and in the rest they are very small. The purest of this Celtic type—*Equus caballus celticus*, as he called it—was from northern Iceland, where the ponies are only 122cm high and, he said, very intelligent.

Ridgeway was more interested in the Arab horse. He noted that this is the only other breed which typically lacks chestnuts on the hindlegs, and has a rather different form of skull and body-build from other horses, with a short back, long thin legs, light head and low snout, and a characteristic dished face. He suggested that here is another basic type, *Equus caballus libycus*.

Of course, like Sanson's, neither of these names has any validity since they are based on ideas, not on animals. Nevertheless the arguments have much merit and the problems they raise have to be faced. Subsequent investigators have failed to take them into account: was there an ancestral wild pony? Was there a wild Arabian horse?

For a long time, however, people rejected such possibilities. Once the existence of a living wild horse, Przewalski's horse (discovered in the 1870s) had been thoroughly digested, people began to realise that it made an unsatisfactory ancestor for domestic horses. This was the basis on which Ewart and Ridgeway argued. But in 1912, Otto Antonius unearthed some old descriptions of the Russian tarpan, in particular Gmelin's description from the eighteenth century; on the basis of these descriptions he dignified the tarpan with a scientific name, *Equus gmelini*, and established its existence as a genuine wild horse from eastern Europe. (Unfortunately he was unaware that soon after Gmelin had written, Boddaert had used the description for the basis of a new name, *Equus ferus*; so that *gmelini* is an exact synonym of *ferus*.) Since what people had been looking for was a second wild horse, more suitable as an ancestor for domestic horses, and preferably found west of the Przewalski horse, this was like manna from heaven. It was seized upon and, almost by default, was placed at the root of all domestic stock; since it was clearly neither Ewart's Celtic horse nor yet Ridgeway's Libyan horse, these latter two were ignored and the theory of multiple origins fell into disrepute.

When the matter was next taken up, in the 1930s, it was along the lines of Ewart and Ridgeway but was rather more comprehensive. The Polish zoologist Skorkowski has written a series of papers from this period up to the present day, supporting the multiple origin theory and creating a series of names for putative wild horses. Some of these names are based on fossil remains, and these therefore belong to real wild horses; others of them, however, like Sanson's, Ewart's and Ridgeway's, are based on constructs. What Skorkowski has done is to measure a large number of domestic horse skulls, separate these into polar types, into which are fitted (if possible) fossil skulls, and propose that these polar types were ancestral subspecies and that living breeds of horses are derived from them by different degrees of interbreeding. There are six polar types in Skorkowski's theory; no breed of horse is a pure-bred descendant of any one of these, but all are cross-bred. Indeed some modern breeds, such as the Arabian and the Turkmenian, are said to result from a crossbreeding of all six!

Among the cross-breds in Skorkowski's theory is the Przewalski horse, derived from four of the six subspecies; the tarpan is derived from the same four, but in different proportions. How this intermixture took place, and where and why, is not explained, and the premise of Skorkowski's theory is questionable.

Not too surprisingly then, Skorkowski's theory made little impact on the Occam's Razor theory, ie domestic horses are descended from a single wild ancestor, and that ancestor was the tarpan. It was not until 1949 that some real evidence on the origin of domestic horses was published.

Bengt Lundholm, a Swedish zoologist, had been studying the skulls of horses dug up in southern Sweden. Some were in deposits dating from Neolithic times or earlier; others were associated with Bronze Age remains. It was not difficult to decide that the Bronze Age horses were domesticated animals; whereas both the period and the deposition circumstances suggested that the earlier remains were of wild horses. None dated from as far back as the

Ice Age: for during the Ice Age, all of Sweden was covered with an ice-sheet. The maximum date was therefore 8000 BC.

In the course of investigating these remains, Lundholm had occasion to examine for comparative purposes a large number of other fossil remains: some other Bronze Age horses from different parts of western Europe, fossils dating from the last Ice Age, and the skeletons of Przewalski horses and tarpans. He soon found that the wild horses could be divided into two groups, one of the best differences being the relative sizes of the second and third molars: an eastern group with M^3 longer than M^2, and a western group with the two teeth the same size. The eastern group contained both the tarpan and Przewalski horse, as well as several fossil types, all of them from east of the Alps: from as far east as the Liakhov Islands of Siberia, to as far west as Nussdorf, near Vienna. The western group in turn divided into two types: a large horse which he called the 'Germanicus group', mainly from the Rhine, and a much smaller type, the 'Microhippus group', typified by a skull from Schussenried in south-western Germany. Horses of the western groups did extend into eastern Europe, and fossil Bohemian and Moravian remains included both eastern and western types.

The point about the distributions was that during the last Ice Age there were ice-sheets over both Scandinavia and the Alps, with just a narrow passage between them. Western Europe was therefore semi-isolated; only animals adapted to extreme cold could get through, and it is likely that in winter it would not have been habitable at all. That western horses, of both types, did occur slightly to the east of the Alps may be a consequence of an improvement of the climate, which is known to have happened twice during the last Ice Age.

Having established the three groups, Lundholm went on to compare his post-glacial Swedish horses with them. They were, he found, of the Germanicus type, but reduced in size. This is reasonable; after the ice had begun to recede there was a period when Sweden was joined by dry land to Denmark, and horses would have spread their range rapidly if the type of habitat was suitable. Among other things there was a small race of horse on Gotland, which was even then an island; probably a few horses had arrived there, swept across by currents from the mainland perhaps, and—as is usual with island races—evolved to a very small size. This must have happened rather quickly—within three or four thousand years.

The Swedish Bronze Age horses showed quite clear evidence of derivation from the Swedish wild horses. Bronze Age horses from other sites in Europe also seemed to be derived from the Germanicus type. On the other hand some early domestic horses, such as a famous series from Etgersleben in Switzerland, were clearly of Microhippus type. Yet other Swiss Bronze Age horses, and most of those from eastern Europe, were of tarpan type; and so are those from Scythian deposits in Central Asia.

This was the first evidence, from hard fossil data, that there were several types of wild horse in Eurasia in the past, and that different types gave rise to domestic types *in situ*. What is more, the evidence suggests that some of these varying types might have been not just races of one species, but actual different species: for their ranges overlapped. Of course, a long time-scale is involved, for the last Ice Age in Europe lasted from about 80,000 to 10,000 years ago, so the presence of three types of wild horse in Czechoslovakian deposits may be because they came in at different times, not because they were all there together. There is, however, some suggestion that at least two types may have coexisted in some places: in the Mendip Caves, in Somerset, whose deposits cover the whole of the last Ice Age, a small type of horse (known from its limb bones) occurs throughout, and in the later deposits is joined by the remains of a larger type of horse. At Solutré in France, a site whose remains have been dated to about 21,000 years ago, there are remains of two thousand or more horses—all limb bones and teeth—which seem to have been intensively hunted by the human inhabitants; the sizes of the bones vary a good deal, and it looks as if there were two species here too, overlapping in size but differing on average.

If there were several species during the Ice Age, capable of living in the same environment without competing for resources and without interbreeding (this we infer from the lack of intermediate specimens), then we can at once see where the heterogeneity of our domestic breeds could have come from. If people domesticated their local varieties of horses and traded them around, then what was suggested for asses becomes even more likely: some horses were found to be better for draft, others for riding, and so on. What is more, the draft horses are likely to have been bred ever more rigorously to be better and better at their tasks; similarly with the riding horses, the sure-footed mountain horses, the sturdy ponies, the racers and the pack horses. So the breeds, starting from different initial potentialities, would diverge more and more. Different types would be interbred, as well as pure-bred; the hybrids were evidently fertile, for cross-breds survive today, and this simply indicates that the species of horse have diverged less than the species of zebra or ass. Again, animals in captivity, forced by man into an unnatural association, will interact in a way they never would in the wild, where they would not even intermingle—and will interbreed.

A new and unexpected light on horse ancestry was shed by Hermann Ebhardt, a horse-breeder in Hamburg: starting not from fossils, nor from the physical characteristics of living horses, but from behaviour. Watching his herds of various breeds as they wandered about their roomy paddocks, observing their reactions to him personally, hypothesising about the sort of environment that would have produced the different behaviours he observed, Ebhardt gradually came to the conclusion that there were four basic patterns—in other words, there must have been four ancestral species. Many breeds showed always the same pattern; in others, different individuals varied in their behaviours. Allying behaviour with the animals' appearance, he then drew his conclusions as to what each of the four would have looked like originally, then turned to fossils: did any fossils seem to correspond with these types?

The answer, according to Ebhardt, was yes: mostly. Some did not correspond exactly, and were put down to wild hybrids—a very dubious solution. Probably the natural variability of a population of wild animals was not fully taken into account; at any rate, I myself see no difficulty in fitting in Ebhardt's 'wild crosses' to one or other of his 'pure species'. More disturbing still is that Ebhardt, like Skorkowski, sees the Przewalski horse as a wild cross-bred. To this suggestion most people would respond: doubtless Przewalski stallions, like tarpan and even mustang stallions, have not been averse to abducting tame mares on occasion, and this may have contributed to the variability of the wild species, but the domestic component would have been weeded out as fast as it was incorporated, being less suited to living under wild conditions. So the Przewalski horse must still be reckoned as a wild species.

It is not at all difficult, taking all this into account, to reconcile Ebhardt's four species with Lundholm's three—there is simply a second species to be added to Lundholm's eastern group, one which he did not consider because its remains hardly occur in Europe. As for Skorkowski's six 'subspecies', some of them can be fitted in quite neatly—not surprisingly, these are the ones based on fossil material!—but others seem to have no real existence.

Ebhardt's Type I is the northern pony: among modern breeds, the Exmoor pony and the Polish peasants' pony, the konik, belong here; and this is, basically, where the Przewalski horse belongs. Since the konik is of this type, we may have no difficulty in seeing its ancestor, the forest tarpan, as a member of this group. It corresponds therefore to Lundholm's eastern group.

The basic name for the species is *Equus ferus*; physically, it is distinguished by having the third molar longer than the second; a broad forehead and narrow snout; a straight profile to the face; short broad cannon-bones; and large nasal cavities.

Northern ponies lived—still live, if so permitted!—in herds of a number of mares, led by a stallion. Young males stay on the periphery of the herd, and leave it when they are sufficiently mature, at 4–5 years. The herds are very compact, and are kept together by the stallion. Among the mares there is a rank-order, determined at least in part by their age, and whether or not they have foals. Within the herd, a mare and her young of different ages make up subgroups. When feeding, the herd move forward together, leaving behind it a wide, grazed 'lawn'. Their reaction to man is one of flight; they all take to their heels against the wind, galloping at first, then perhaps slowing down to a trot or pace. Finally they stop, under some shelter, and turn to look back and investigate.

Clearly this was an open-country form originally—perhaps, as Ebhardt suggests, a tundra species. The teeth are high-crowned with thick enamel, implying very hard-wearing plant foods. They probably made long seasonal migrations to find suitable pastures.

The northern ponies seem to have divided early on into three groups—three ecotypes as they may be called: one on the tundra, one in the open forests, one on the steppe. At least the steppe and forest groups can be traced back to the last interglacial period, between 120,000 and 80,000 years ago, and their subsequent evolution can also be traced. Each of these ecotypes seems to have evolved along broadly similar lines, implying that they continued to interbreed where their ranges met.

The steppe group of northern ponies were medium-sized animals with large teeth and long snouts. The steppe tarpan decreased in size during its evolution: last interglacial representatives were 160–5cm high, those in the early part of the last Ice Age were 144cm, those from the latter half were 136–7cm, and the recent (post-glacial) tarpan was only 130cm high. The eastern race, the Przewalski horse (which has larger teeth than the tarpan) is 140cm high today, and seems to have diminished less than the tarpan.

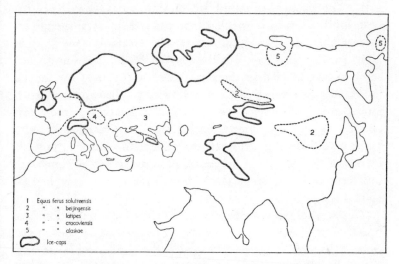

Fig 11 *Known distribution of subspecies* Equus ferus, *the northern pony, in the late Würm glaciation (about 20,000 years ago)*

The forest group lived not in the coniferous forest of Siberia, but in the open, mixed forests—or parkland region—of eastern Europe. They have always been smaller than the steppe representatives, with smaller teeth, but much less on the whole is known about them. They too decreased in size, from 150cm height in the last interglacial to about 120cm in recent times.

The tundra group was different from both of the other two types, but we know little about its evolution because we cannot be sure of the dates of the remains from Alaska or the Liakhov Islands (Siberia); they are most likely recent—after the last Ice Age—for the Liakhov Islands are thought to have been under ice before that. They were certainly very short-snouted, with rather small teeth, and about 135–40cm high. This type is represented in Europe too; the late Ice Age horses from Solutre included some individuals of this type, and it survives in more or less pure form in the Exmoor pony.

It is interesting that in both steppe and tundra types the European forms seem to be smaller than the Asiatic ones: the tarpan smaller than the Przewalski horse, the Exmoor pony (125cm high) smaller than the Siberian/Alaskan horse. Colours do not seem to have varied in the same way, however: of the steppe horses, the Przewalski horse is yellowish red-brown, the tarpan mouse-grey, both having a dorsal stripe and dark legs; the forest tarpan was grey, apparently turning white in winter; the tundra horse of Siberia was evidently white, but the Exmoor pony is brown. The evidence of the mane, even in tarpans, is equivocal, but there is no reason to think that all races must have had an erect mane.

On the whole, this species has had little effect on the domestic horse. Some Asiatic breeds, as one would expect, are descended from it (like the Turkmen pony), so is the konik, and it has contributed to the stock of the Hanoverian horse, the Icelandic pony, many British ponies, and the ancient wild Dülmer breed.

Ebhardt's Type II can be called the northern great horse, *Equus woldrichi*; this is the second eastern type, the one not distinguished by Lundholm, although its remains have been found in some sites in eastern Europe from the last Ice Age—as far west as Austria where it occurs in such sites as Nussdorf, near Vienna, and at Salzgitter-Lebenstedt; its remains occur alongside those of the northern pony in Siberia, along the Yana river. It was extremely large—large enough to be always easily distinguishable from Type I, but like it, decreased in size with time. It had a rather short snout, a narrow forehead, and small teeth, with big nasal cavities like Type I; basically it was a tundra species: Ebhardt specifies gravel-tundra, swampy in summer and snowy in winter, and he observes that this is the only type of horse that can stand in swamp and feed on submerged plants with its nose in icy water.

Type II horses have a looser herd structure than Type I; the stallion is usually rather peripheral and stands downwind of the herd, staying near it, but joining it only in the rutting season. The mares have a strict rank-order, maintained by threat gestures, and when the stallion approaches the herd he is challenged by the leading mare. Young females remain in the herd; young males leave it, staying nearby under the supervision of the herd stallion. When feeding, the herd spreads out, leaving streaks of cropped grass as the animals move about.

When a man approaches the herd, the animals bunch together with their necks outstretched towards the intruder; as he comes near, they shrink away, jumping backwards and sideways, and turn to flee, against the wind, with the stallion at the rear. Ebhardt interprets this as being an attempt at camouflage in the initial stages.

The representatives of this species that lived in the last inter-glacial were huge, standing 170–80cm high; those from the last Ice Age were slightly smaller, averaging 170cm; in latest glacial and early post-glacial times they were considerably smaller, 148–54cm high. How long they survived is uncertain, but their remains have been found in post-glacial deposits in Moravia and Russia. Ebhardt says that this type, like the last, did not have much influence on the domestic horse; some Russian breeds are derived from it, and those known as cold-bloods, as well as the large type of Icelandic horse, the Highland-Garron, the Devon packhorse and some others. The species seems not to have lived wild in western Europe (west of the Alps), nor in North America, unless the very big teeth referred to '*Equus giganteus*' belong to it.

The Type III horse is the one Lundholm called the Germanicus type, with the third molar no larger than the second, a very narrow forehead, long snout, relatively small teeth, straight jaw, and long limbs. It was a fresh-plant grazer, with teeth adapted to cropping, and lived in marsh and woodland areas in central Europe during the last Ice Age, and probably previous ones; unlike the previous two species it was probably a sedentary form occupying year-round pastures. The social group consisted of a mare with her female offspring; and although these might have aggregated together, there was little or no herd tendency. The stallion would visit the herd only during the rutting season, and young males associated together in bachelor bands. When feeding, the female-young herds graze within a tight area, leaving a spreading patch of cropped grass; these pastures were strenuously defended against other groups.

The reaction to man in this species is based on defence as much as flight. The mare of the group stands watching the intruder,

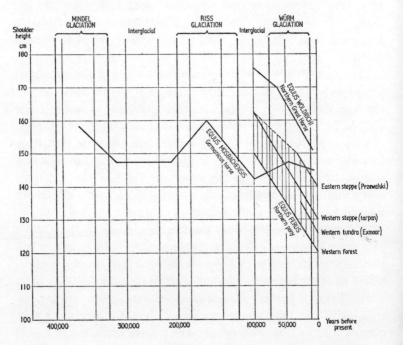

Fig 12   *Variations in size through time of three species of wild horse*

suddenly laying her ears back, pawing the ground, tossing her head and moving slightly to one side; as the intruder comes nearer, she snaps her jaws audibly, and prepares to defend herself and her group with teeth and hooves.

This species was evidently always restricted to Europe, its remains being especially common in the Rhineland which seems always to have offered a suitable habitat, come ice age or warm spell. The abundance of its remains make it a very well-known type, and its continuous evolution can be taken back as far as the second of the four glaciations, perhaps 400,000 years ago. What this probably means is that those of the last (fourth) Ice Age, contemporary with Type I in Europe, were little-changed descendants of the big Mosbach horse, the most primitive and earliest fossil horse that has been substantiated—and that the other three species have diverged considerably from it. If we take the story back to Mosbach, then we find that this type, from the second glaciation, averaged 158cm high; those in the succeeding interglacial were 145–50cm high; in the third Ice Age, larger again, 155–65cm; in the last interglacial 141–5cm; in the last Ice Age 145–50cm; and in post-glacial times, 142–8cm for the Swedish wild horses and 153cm for the wild horses of Lake Ladoga on the Russian–Finnish border. The story is more or less one of larger horses in the ice ages, smaller ones in the warm periods, but with a gradual overall decrease none the less. The teeth also decreased, but seem to have been always one step behind the body size, so that there were 'harmonic' and 'disharmonic' proportions succeeding one another.

The Germanicus horse has left numerous domestic descendants, pure-bred and crossed. In general, these are the heavy horses Kladruber, Holsteiner, Flemish, Percheron, Hanoverian warmbloods with the bass-fiddle head; all doubtless altered considerably in one way or another, but all showing similar behaviour and the basic physical characteristics of the species.

Type IV, on the other hand, is poorly known as a fossil, but its domestic descendants are well known and easily distinguished. It is a medium-to-small horse, about 130cm high, with a medium-to-broad forehead, short broad snout, dished face, straight jaw, and low-crowned teeth but a long tooth row so that the teeth seem to be too large for the jaw. This originated as a subtropical type, in high rainfall areas. The stallion lives permanently with one or a few females and their offspring, forming a family herd similar to, but smaller, than the Type I herd. The grazing pattern seems to be one of steady grazing for a short distance; the animal then walks forward and begins grazing again. The reaction to man is, like Type I, one of flight; the stallion urges the others on with his teeth, and the whole group takes to flight against the wind.

It is difficult to avoid the conclusion that this type is related to Type I; its behaviour is very similar, but its skull and teeth are rather different. Unfortunately it is poorly known as a fossil, but the complete skull from the late Ice Age site of Schussenried belongs to this type. Its modern representatives include the Celtic ponies—the small Icelandic, the Shetland, and the Faeroese—the Fjord ponies of Norway, the Arab horse, and the Togo pony of West Africa. It thus includes both Ewart's *celticus* and Ridgeway's *libycus*, and doubtless there were northern and southern geographic races which would have given rise to these two types. Basing ourselves on Ewart's findings, we can suggest that this species may have lacked chestnuts on the hindlimbs, and perhaps also may have had a short-haired tail root like some races, at least, of *Equus ferus*.

Except for Type I, whose living and recent wild representatives are well known, it is difficult to say what names these horse species should bear. In former times, people would dig up a new fossil skull and, with gay abandon, give it a name as if it were a new species. Some of these names are based on such fragmentary material that it is doubtful whether we will ever know what sort of horse they represented; others are founded on better data, such as complete skulls, but have been misused. The skull from Unkelstein, near Remagen, was baptised *Equus germanicus* by its discoverer, Nehring, but the name has been so misused that no one is clear any more what it means. It is perhaps lucky that this was a name given earlier by Sanson to one of his constructs, which prevents it being used for any other type, and the name must fall into disuse, although there is nothing wrong with informally speaking of the Germanicus type as Lundholm does. In 1902, Reichenau described the big Middle Pleistocene horse *Equus mosbachensis*, and since the Germanicus horse can be traced back in an unbroken line to this form, and changed comparatively little, this is the suitable name for the species as a whole.

The Schussenried horse and its relatives have never received a valid scientific name at all; but a good informal name for them would be Lundholm's Microhippus type.

As for the huge horses of Type II, it must be revealed that for some inscrutable reason the palaeontologist Woldřich, who described the remains from Nussdorf in 1882, dubbed them 'Equus caballus fossilis minor'; it is certainly a matter for relief that four-part names are ineligible for scientific consideration—imagine the biggest species of horse being called 'Equus minor'! —and that the first proper name for this species is the quite inoffensive, if non-specific, *Equus woldrichi*.

But the important point about all this is that the four-species theory makes sense; on grounds of the animals' appearance, behaviour, ecology and fossil history. It untangles the threads, and shows the way round the difficulty of trying to derive such diverse types as carthorses, Arab horses and ponies from a single stock.

As for what the four types looked like, clothed with skin and hair, in their wild state—who knows? We have the Przewalski horse and the Exmoor pony, alive and well; we have good descriptions of the tarpan, and indications of the Lamut wild horse. But these all belong to Type I, *Equus ferus*. Ewart, Ridgeway and

Skorkowski, among others, have tried to reconstruct the likely colour and conformation of various other wild progenitor types, but all such attempts must remain speculative. There remains the evidence of the people who lived alongside the wild horses: pictorial evidence, carved on stone and ivory, painted on the walls of caves, in south-western France and northern Spain, from 30,000–10,000 BC.

At first sight, cave art is disappointing as evidence of the true appearance of a species, as there is such obvious artistic license. There are of course exceptions: there is the marvellous and exact horse from Niaux, with its shaggy coat, thick head, bearded chops and upright mane, with nostrils, lips, eyes, all picked out with care and artistry. In such a case, there is little doubt that the artist was depicting the local tundra horse, *Equus ferus solutreensis*, and in any case only the northern pony is known with any certainty as a fossil from the Franco-Cantabrian area where this form of cave art flourished. This has not prevented several authors from finding a whole galaxy of horse species and subspecies represented on cave walls, defined by colour, head shape, body form, limb length and so on—all surely subject to the greatest artistic license.

None the less, there are one or two interesting conclusions which can, I think, validly be derived from these sources. One concerns the mane. If one has seen only Przewalski horses with upright manes, then surely one does not imagine a hanging or flowing mane out of the top of one's head? Yet a falling mane, such as characterises most domestic horses, can be found, though rarely, in Franco-Cantabrian art, such as on the horse at Le Portel, remarkable for its rhythm and movement in its execution. I would conclude from this that there must have been a type of horse with a flowing mane, living in that region at that time: probably, to judge from the ratio of erect to falling manes (about 10:1) a rather scarce species. *Equus mosbachensis*, perhaps?

Then there are the much discussed horses of Peche-Merle;

two little fellows standing back-to-back, their rumps overlapping, with ridiculous short legs but graceful, sweeping necks and heads and, again, falling mane and forelock depicted in a darker colour. They are covered all over with dark dots. Are these dots, perhaps, of magical significance, as the Abbé Breuil insisted? Or does the scene represent a myth of the time? Or are the animals ikons in a shrine, as Leroi-Gourhan thinks? Each of these interpretations might make one deny that the dots could be a realistic representation; but Erna Mohr has noted that many elderly horses assume, if briefly, a dapple-grey coat, and that the rarity of such animals might make them a subject of ritual significance.

THE FUTURE

Horses and donkeys have served us well. But what future have they? I think that once we in the West recognise that machines have limitations, they will once again find a place in our society and our employment. Indeed, in Great Britain, Shire horses are already on the way back. Grévy's zebra, or at least its hybrids with horses, looks as if it may have a future in the service of man in East Africa. Burchell's zebra, on the other hand, may have no specific use except as part of the plains ecosystem. However, it will be there, ready for the cameras of the tourists, or if need be will help to provide protein for starving villagers, living as it does on arid savannah land that may be soon rendered sterile by farming or cattle-keeping.

But what of the mountain zebra? It is not numerous enough to be a source of food, nor has it yet been domesticated. The problem is survival itself. And I think we should be concerned with its survival, together with that of the onager, the kiang, and the African wild ass. They must not be permitted to go the way of the quagga. They are being constantly pressed on all sides by cultivation, by the need for land for stock-rearing, by projects to 'make the desert bloom', by road-building, by new settlements, by all the novelties of modernisation, and by the need to cope with an ever-expanding human population.

'Don't worry; we can grow enough food to feed everybody'; how often have we heard that from apologists for pro-natalism? Even if it is true—and it is noteworthy that an agronomist rarely gives such an optimistic viewpoint—it misses the point in a way. The problem of remaining alive is one thing; the question of living one's life to the full, of enjoyment and fulfilment, is quite another. For an increasing number of people, in underdeveloped countries as well as in developed ones, wildlife is a major part of that enjoyment. People who have never seen a wild ass derive pleasure simply from knowing that there are such things; and to hear that their existence is threatened, not by deliberate malice but by necessity, because their habitat is needed to feed or house the human surplus, causes despair. For this reason alone, human beings must curb their fertility; such a suggestion is regarded by some people as blasphemy, but to wipe out a species, a unique product of creation—that surely is the ultimate blasphemy.

Appendices

1 CLASSIFICATION OF THE GENUS *EQUUS*

SUBGENUS *Dolichohippus*

Equus shoshonensis   3·5m BP,[1] North America
  „   *robustus*   3–1m BP, Eurasia and North America
  „   *stenonis* $2\frac{1}{2}$–1m BP, southern Europe
  „   *suessenbornensis*   500,000 BP, Europe
  „   *cautleyi* $2\frac{1}{2}$m BP (uncertain), India
  „   *sanmeniensis*   2m BP (uncertain), China
  „   *valeriani*   100,000 BP, Uzbekistan
  „   *plicatus* $2\frac{1}{2}$–1m BP, South and East Africa
  „   *grevyi*   Recent, North-east Africa   Grévy's zebra

SUBGENUS *Hippotigris*

Equus sellardsi   3·5m BP, North America
  „   *helmei*   1m BP, South Africa
  „   *zebra*   Recent (and fossil), South Africa   mountain zebra
  „   *quagga*   Recent (and fossil), South Africa   quagga
  „   *burchelli*   Recent (and fossil), South and East Africa   Burchell's
        zebra

SUBGENUS *Amerhippus*

Equus fraternus   400,000–200,000 BP, North America
  „   *complicatus*   200,000–100,000 BP, North America
  „   *occidentalis*   100,000–10,000 BP, North America
  „   *andium*   400,000–200,000 BP, Andes Mountains
  „   *neogaeus*   200,000–10,000 BP, Argentina

[1] ie 3.5 million years before present

SUBGENUS *Asinus*

Equus stehlini   1m BP, Italy
  „   *hydruntinus*   200,000–5,000 BP, Europe
  „   *graziosii*   50,000 BP, Italy
  „   *conversidens*   200,000–10,000 BP, North America
  „   *sivalensis*   500,000 BP (uncertain), India
  „   *kiang*   Recent, Tibet and Ladakh   kiang
  „   *hemionus*   Recent (and fossil), Asia   onager
  „   *africanus*   Recent, North Africa   African wild ass

SUBGENUS *Equus*

Equus simionescui   1·5m BP (uncertain), Rumania
  „   *scotti*   200,000–10,000 BP, North America
  „   *laurentius*   200,000–10,000 BP, North America
  „   *mosbachensis*   400,000–Recent, western Europe   Germanicus horse
  „   *woldrichi*   100,000–Recent, eastern Europe and northern Asia   northern great horse
  „   *ferus*   100,000–Recent, northern Eurasia and Alaska   northern pony
  „   *sp?*   30,000–Recent, western Europe   Microhippus horse

2 SPECIES OF EQUIDS: SOME STATISTICS

	ferus	*kiang*	*hemionus*	*africanus*	*zebra*	*quagga*	*burchelli*	*grevyi*
Height (cm) (large, medium, small races)	140	140 holdereri 135 kiang 110 polyodon	130 {hemionus, luteus, kulan} 120 {onager, khur} 100 hemippus	129 somaliensis 122 africanus	130 hartmannae 120 zebra	132	135 S Africa 125 E Africa	150
Head length, percentage of height	41	41	40	40	38	40	40	40
Metacarpal to radius length	68%	77	71·7	67	67	69	76	70
Metacarpal to metatarsal length	84–5	85–7	85–7	83–5	87–8	87	89–90	87
Hooves	broad	broad	narrow	very narrow	very narrow	narrow	broad	broad
Number of lumbar vertebrae	5–6	5	5	5	5	6	6	6
Wolf tooth, retained	no	yes	no	no	yes	no	no (S Africa) yes (E Africa)	no
Chromosome number	66	?	54–6	62	32	?	44	46
Gestation (days)	335	355	368	365	371	?	371	390
Infundibulum, lower incisors	yes	yes	yes	yes	yes	yes	no (E Africa) yes (S Africa)	yes
Chestnuts on hindlimbs	yes	no	no	no	no	no	no	no
Ratio of intestine length to height	15:1	?	12:1	11:1	17·5:1	?	17·5:1	11·5:1
Total world population	196	several thousand	ditto	1,000[1]	5,000–8,000[2]	0	300,000	several thousand

[1] Almost all of the subspecies *somaliensis*

[2] Almost all of the subspecies *hartmannae*

3 *EQUUS FERUS* (NORTHERN PONY): VARIANTS IN TIME AND SPACE

1 Open-country type (steppe and tundra): broad forehead, short snout, large size, large teeth.
   A Tundra forms: shorter snout, smaller teeth.
>   Eastern type: larger size, colour white. Northern Siberia, Alaska.
>>   Würm glacial: height 135–40cm. *Equus ferus alaskae.*
>>   Postglacial: ?Lamut wild horse.
>   Western type: smaller size, colour brown (?). Western Europe.
>>   Würm glacial: height 136–8cm. *Equus ferus solutreensis.*
>>   Postglacial: height 125cm. Exmoor pony.
   B Steppe forms: longer snout, larger teeth.
>   Eastern type: larger size, larger teeth, colour red-yellow. China, Mongolia.
>>   Würm glacial: height 150cm. *Equus ferus beijingensis.*
>>   Postglacial: height 140cm. *Equus ferus przewalskii.*
>   Western type: smaller size, smaller teeth, colour grey. Eastern Europe.
>>   Riss-Würm interglacial: height 160–5cm. *Equus ferus chosaricus.*
>>   Early Würm glacial: height 144cm. *Equus ferus latipes* (early form).
>>   Late Würm glacial: height 136–7cm. *Equus ferus latipes* (late form).
>>   Postglacial: height 130cm. *Equus ferus ferus,* tarpan.

2 Forest type: narrow forehead, long snout, small size, small teeth. Eastern Europe.
>   Riss-Würm interglacial: height 150cm. *Equus ferus missi.*
>   Würm glacial: height 139cm. *Equus ferus cracoviensis.*
>   Postglacial: height 120cm. *Equus ferus silvestris.*

4 GEOGRAPHICAL VARIATIONS IN WILD ASSES AND ZEBRAS

All members of a species are clearly recognisable as members of that species, but at the same time those in one area may differ somewhat from those in another. Thus, kiangs all over their range are recognisably kiangs, but those in south-eastern Tibet are smaller than those elsewhere; those in Ladakh and western Tibet are darker than all others. These distinct, geographical types are called subspecies; they are given names by adding a word on to the end of the species name. The subspecies which was the first to be discovered (so the one to which the species' name was originally given) is called the nominate subspecies: the third word in its name is a repetition of the specific name. The kiang was first discovered in the 1830s in Ladakh and named *Equus kiang*; the other subspecies were discovered and named later, so the Ladakh subspecies is called *Equus kiang kiang*.

SUBSPECIES OF *EQUUS KIANG*

1   *Equus kiang kiang*. Western kiang. Extreme western Tibet; Ladakh. Very dark colour; 135cm high.

2   *Equus kiang holdereri*. Eastern kiang. Kukunor, and north-eastern part of Tibetan plateau. Light colour; 140cm high.

3   *Equus kiang polyodon*. Southern kiang. Region north of Sikkim. Light colour; 110cm high.

SUBSPECIES OF *EQUUS HEMIONUS*

1   *Equus hemionus hemionus*. North Mongolian dziggetai. Transbaikalia, North Mongolia, Dzungaria to eastern Kazakhstan. Disruptive coloration; dorsal stripe with white border; 130cm high.

2   *Equus hemionus luteus*. Gobi dziggetai. Gobi desert. Intergrading coloration; no white border to dorsal stripe; 130cm high.

3   *Equus hemionus kulan*. Kulan. Turkmenia. Fairly intergrading pattern; white border (as in all succeeding subspecies); 120cm high.

4   *Equus hemionus onager*. Ghor-khar. Iran. More disruptive, darker colour than preceding subspecies; thinner winter coat; 120cm high.

5   *Equus hemionus khur*. Khur. Thar desert, India/Pakistan border re-

gion. Greyer than preceding forms; more white on flanks; short winter coat; dorsal stripe does not reach tail-tip; 120cm high.

6 *Equus hemionus hemippus*. Achdari. Syrian desert. Intergrading pattern; little white on flanks; short winter coat; 100cm high.

SUBSPECIES OF *EQUUS AFRICANUS*

1 *Equus africanus africanus*. Nubian wild ass. Reddish-grey; shoulder-cross but no leg-stripes; 122cm high.

2 *Equus africanus somaliensis*. Somali wild ass. Buff grey; leg-stripes but usually no shoulder-stripe; 129cm high.

SUBSPECIES OF *EQUUS BURCHELLI*

1 *Equus burchelli burchelli*. Burchell's zebra. Orange Free State and north-east Cape Province. Buff with white belly and legs; stripes narrow, not reaching midline of belly; legs unstriped; shadow-stripes; 135cm high.

2 *Equus burchelli antiquorum*. Damara zebra. Southern Angola, northern Namibia, Botswana, Transvaal and Natal. Differs in that stripes reach midline of belly, and extend down legs as far as knees and hocks; shadow-stripes; 135cm high.

3 *Equus burchelli chapmanni*. Chapman's zebra. Rhodesia and southern Mozambique, south of the Zambesi. Differs in that leg-stripes reach nearly to hooves but are broken and incomplete; 135cm high.

4 *Equus burchelli zambeziensis*. Upper Zambesi zebra. Zambia, west of Muchinga escarpment, eastern Angola, south-east Zaire. Legs fully striped; shadow-stripes faint or absent; ground colour yellowish; skull has an elongated braincase; 125cm high.

5 *Equus burchelli crawshayi*. Crawshay's zebra. Mozambique north of the Zambesi, Malawi, Zambia east of Muchinga escarpment. Legs fully striped; ground colour white or buff; shadow-stripes faint or absent; very narrow, close striping; 125cm high.

6 *Equus burchelli boehmi*. Grant's zebra. Tanzania, Kenya, into Uganda, Rwanda, Sudan, Ethiopia and Somalia. Legs fully striped; ground colour white; shadow-stripes faint or absent; stripes very broad, sometimes (on hindquarters) broader than white interspaces; mane often poorly developed; 125cm high.

SUBSPECIES OF *EQUUS ZEBRA*

1 *Equus zebra zebra*. Cape mountain zebra. Mountains of Cape Province. Stocky build, longer ears; stripes very broad, broader than white interspaces; ground colour white; 120cm high.

2 *Equus zebra hartmannae*. Hartmann's zebra. Mountains coastal zone of Namibia and southern Angola. Taller, shorter ears; stripes narrow, with broader interspaces; ground colour buff; 130cm high.

Index

Achdari, 101, 115, 188
Amerhippus, 48, 121, 183
Anchitheriinae, 40
Artiodactyla, 19
Asinus, 29, 30, 31, 184
   palestinae, 117
Askaniya Nova, 34, 51, 63
Ass, 25, 26, 28, 34, 43, 46
  domestic, *see* Donkey
  wild:
    African, 31, 32, 46, 106–14, 161–2
    Indian, 99
    Nubian, 109, 110, 112, 113, 115, 188
    Persian, 100, 105
    Somali, 16, 109, 110, 111, 188
    Syrian, 14, 101
    Tibetan, 87
    Turkmenian, 100

Boddaert, 69
Boswall, J., 111
Brumbie, 77–8
Burro, 118

Camargue, 81
Catskill Game Park, 52, 57
Cyrus the Great, 37

Dinohippus, 44
Dobroruka, L. J., 64
Dolichohippus, 29, 31, 44, 45, 46, 47, 48, 123
Donkey, 14, 39, 114–17, 161–2
Dziggetai, 98, 99, 187

Ebhardt, H., 84, 170–8
Eoequus, 44
Eohippus, 39
Epihippus, 40
Equus, 28, 29, 49, 183, 184
  africanus, 29, 106, 119, 184, 185
    africanus, 120, 188
    palestinae, 117, 120, 162
    somaliensis, 117, 188
  aluticus, 47
  andium, 48, 183
  asinus, 39, 160
    atlanticus, 114
  burchelli, 29, 124, 183, 185
    antiquorum, 188
    boehmi, 188
    burchelli, 188
    chapmanni, 188
    crawshayi, 188
    zambeziensis, 188
  caballus, 39, 160
  cautleyi, 45, 183
  complicatus, 122, 183
  conversidens, 47, 121, 122, 184
  ferus, 29, 69, 166, 172, 179, 184, 185
    alaskae, 76, 186
    beijingensis, 186
    chosaricus, 186
    cracoviensis, 186
    ferus, 69, 186
    latipes, 186
    missi, 186
    przewalskii, 69, 186
    solutreensis, 180, 186
    sylvaticus, 70

Equus ferus—contd
 sylvestris, 70, 186
fraternus, 48, 122, 183
germanicus, 179
giganteus, 175
gmelini, 69, 166
graziosii, 119, 184
grevyi, 29, 153, 183, 185
helmei, 183
hemionus, 29, 96, 120, 184, 185
 hemippus, 162, 188
 hemionus, 187
 khur, 187
 kulan, 187
 luteus, 187
 nipponicus, 121
 onager, 187
 ordosensis, 121
hydruntinus, 119, 121, 184
kiang, 29, 88, 184, 185
 holdereri, 187
 kiang, 187
 polyodon, 187
lambei, 76
laurentius, 184
mauritanicus, 137
mosbachensis, 47, 179, 180, 184
neogaeus, 183
niobrarensis alaskae, 75
occidentalis, 48, 122, 183
plicatus, 46, 153, 183
quagga, 29, 183, 185
robustus, 45, 47, 123, 153, 183
sanmeniensis, 45, 183
scotti, 47, 75, 184
sellardsi, 183
shoshonensis, 183
simionescui, 47, 184
simplicidens, 45, 153
sivalensis, 47, 121, 184
steblini, 47, 121, 184
stenonsis, 45, 47, 121, 123, 153, 183
suessenbornensis, 45, 183
tabeti, 47
tscherskii, 75
valeriani, 45, 154, 183
woldrichi, 174, 179, 184
zebra, 29, 137, 183, 185

greatheadi, 139
 hartmannae, 189
 zebra, 189
Ewart, J. C., 165

Gee, E. P., 105
Germanicus, 175-7
Ghor-khar, 100, 103, 115, 187
Gmelin, 66, 69, 166
Grzimek, B., 135-6

Haflinger, 81
Harrison, D., 116
Hay, O., 75-6
Hedin, S., 98
Heck, L. and H., 70-1
Hemionus, 30
Heptner, V. G., 66, 68, 99
Herodotus, 69, 73
Hipparion, 42
Hippotigris, 29, 31, 45, 46, 47, 48, 123
Hinny, 33
Hook, R., 33
Horse, 26, 43, 44, 46
 domestic, 13, 14, 28, 31, 39, 165-81
 Lamut wild, 74, 85
 North African wild, 77
 Przewalski, 14, 26, 31, 34, 50-66, 73, 84, 85, 171, 173, 174
Hyracotherium, 39

Infundibulum, 23, 24, 25

Jewell, J., 159

Keast, J. A., 156-7
Khur, 101, 103, 115, 187
Kiang, 16, 31, 86-96, 103, 104, 181, 187
Klingel, H., 124, 132, 133, 134, 135, 139, 145, 154
Kulan, 100-1, 103, 115, 187

Lundholm, B., 139, 167-9, 171

McKnight, T., 80
Mark, *see* Infundibulum
Mason, M., 113
Mazák, V., 51, 63

Microhippus, 168
Millar, J. G. C., 142, 145, 147
Mohr, E., 57, 105
Mule, 33, 34, 35
Mustang, 79–80

Neanderthal man, 45, 120

Onager, 16, 31, 96–106, 162–4, 181
Orohippus, 40

Perissodactyla, 19
Pfizenmayr, E., 74
Pliny the Elder, 69
Plesippus, 44
Pony:
  Connemara, 81, 82–3
  Dales, 81, 83
  Dartmoor, 81, 83
  Exmoor, 81, 84–5, 174, 186
  Fells, 81, 83
  Highland, 81, 82, 83
  New Forest, 81, 83
  Northern, 171, 184
  Shetland, 81, 82
  Welsh, 81
Powell-Cotton, P. H. G., 113
Prague zoo, 50–2, 57, 63
Pruski, W., 66–7

Quagga, 14, 148–52, 181, 183, 185
Quinn, J. H., 43, 44, 122

Radulesco and Samson, 47
Rhinoceros, 15, 20, 40
Ridgeway, W., 165–6

Samson, C., 165–6
Schäfer, E., 88, 94
Simpson, G. G., 43
Skorkowski, E., 167, 171, 180
Smith, C. H., 67
Speed, J. G., 84
Solomatin, A. O., 99, 105

Tapir, 20, 40
Tarpan, 14, 66–73, 85, 172–3, 186
Teeth, 21–5
Thesiger, W., 115–16

Vetulani, 70
Volf, J., 57

Zebra, 25, 28, 43, 44, 124
  Böhm's, 124
  Burchell's, 16, 25, 26, 31, 32, 34, 46,
    48, 124–37, 138, 150, 151, 156–7,
    181, 188
  Cape mountain, 15, 138, 141, 142,
    145–9, 189
  Chapman's, 127, 188
  Crawshay's, 124–7, 188
  Damara, 127, 188
  Grant's, 124, 136, 188
  Grévy's, 16, 25, 31, 32, 33, 34, 44, 45,
    46, 48, 123, 136, 152–7, 181, 183
  Hartmann's, 16, 138, 140, 141, 189
  Mountain, 14, 31, 32, 136, 137–48, 183
  Upper Zambesi, 127, 188
  Wahlberg's, 127